JUSTICE,
JUSTICE

A JEWISH VIEW OF
THE BLACK REVOLUTION

Justice, justice shalt thou pursue.

Deuteronomy 16:20

Why is the word justice written twice? To teach us that we must practice justice at all times—whether it be for our profit or for our loss, and towards all men—towards Jews and non-Jews alike.

Tanhuma

JUSTICE, JUSTICE

A JEWISH VIEW OF
THE BLACK REVOLUTION

by RABBI HENRY COHEN

BM
538
N3
C 67

108538

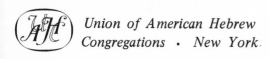 Union of American Hebrew
Congregations • New York.

Library of Congress Catalogue Card Number 68-31152

Revised 1969

Copyright 1968

by the

UNION OF AMERICAN HEBREW CONGREGATIONS

New York, N. Y.

Produced in the United States of America

Lincoln was fond of telling the story about four white men scrubbing a Negro in a potash kettle filled with cold water. The men thought that by scrubbing him they might make him white. Just about the time they thought they were succeeding, he caught cold and died.

Approximately a century later, a young man wrote: "If you ostracize me because I am unclean, I can cleanse myself. If you segregate me because I am ignorant, I can become educated. But if you discriminate against me because of my color, I can do nothing. God gave me my color, I can do nothing. I have no possible protection but to take refuge in cynicism, bitterness, hatred, and despair."

Tragically but understandably, the black American has resorted to such refuge in vast numbers. The mounting problem which we have created over the years is basically a moral one. The black man must be rescued not only from his ghetto but from his despair and degradation.

There has been great need for an elucidation of Jewish values in relation to the racial issues which threaten to rend the social fabric. Our students are deeply concerned about racial discrimination and are questioning the relevance of Judaism as a vital response to the problem.

What is the relationship of Jewish tradition to the racial issue? How can the Jew respond to the moral questions involved in the issue *qua* Jew? Does Judaism provide a unique outlook? If Jews have been in the vanguard of the civil rights struggle, what accounts for Negro anti-Semitism? These are the essential questions to which Rabbi Henry Cohen addresses himself in this penetrating study. We are happy to bring his contribution to our students for use both in high school and adult education programs.

Jack D. Spiro

PREFACE TO REVISED EDITION

When *Justice, Justice* was written, it was understood that revisions would have to be made from time to time, if the text were to deal with those issues of current concern posed by the Black Revolution. It was not, however, foreseen how far-reaching the revisions would have to be within the period of but one year. Yet, from June 1968 to June 1969, the Black Revolution entered a new phase, especially in its relation to the Jewish community.

There was first the Civil Rights movement, the struggle for equality under the law, when "black and white together" joined hands to overcome discrimination from places of public accommodation to the ballot box. Then there was the shocking realization that equality in theory did not mean equality in fact, for the enemy more obstinate even than discriminatory laws was the social and economic conditions that meant poverty and the end of hope for millions of blacks. The unwillingness or inability of the nation to enable the poor to lift themselves out of the quicksand of slum life led to the angry, frustrated cry for black power. All this was discussed in the first edition.

But since the first edition was written, the cluster of separatist, nationalist, and radical ideas vaguely associated with the cry for black power has become, to a degree, crystallized into an ideology and strategy for black self-determination. This ideology considers integration a naive dream and advocates black community control of those institutions that affect the lives of black people. The strategy is one of confrontation, in which Jewish merchants and teachers may find their interests in conflict with the interests of the self-determinists. Out of this conflict there has arisen bitter criticism of the Jewish community, labeled anti-Semitism by most Jews but believed justified by many blacks.

The impact of this new mood has shattered the confidence of many Jews in the liberal assumption that blacks and Jews are natural allies, both being minority groups. In some sections of America, notably Brooklyn, they are behaving more in the manner of adversaries. Not only is the conventional wisdom of the liberal being challenged but the

[vii]

moral commitment of Judaism to the struggle for true equality of opportunity is being called into question: "Why should we help them when they hate us?"

In view of these new developments, not only has the first edition of *Justice, Justice* been "updated" but a supplementary section has been added which poses the question, "Allies or Adversaries?" Chapter Six, "Black Self-Determination and Jewish Nationalism" compares and contrasts the new movement in the black community with various Jewish movements towards self-determination. Chapter Seven, "Community Control and the Right to Power," explores the various strategies being proposed to achieve self-determination with the emphasis on community control of schools and a secondary stress on autonomous higher education for blacks. Chapter Eight, "A New Look at Black Anti-Semitism" integrates the last chapter of the first edition with an analysis of the debate currently raging over anti-Jewish feeling in the black community: What is its extent? What are its causes? How dangerous is it? How should Jews respond?

There could hardly be a greater mistake than to view this latest phase of the Black Revolution as an isolated social phenomenon. Black self-determination and its challenge to the Jewish and general community can be understood only in relation to the prior phases of the revolt. In fact, the issues raised by the Civil Rights movement and the war against poverty and dealt with in the first edition are still very much alive. These are the very issues that the white community should be confronting: What strategies for social change should be adopted in America? Why should one care about the rights of his fellow man? Who or what is responsible for the high proportion of poor within the black community? Shall we give up on the system or are there realistic programs that can enable the black man to enter into the mainstream of American life?

All these questions are explored in Chapters Two through Five where they are viewed in the light of Jewish belief and experience. The author's understanding of "a Jewish view" is set forth in the first chapter. In general terms, this text is an attempt to build a bridge between the objective world of factual knowledge and the normative world of moral commitment. Too often religionists are content to voice general ethical principles, which each "believer" proceeds to apply in ways that are harmonious with his own particular opinions and prejudices. Too often secularists present all the facts without ever confronting the real moral choices or the values which guide them in making those choices. *Justice, Justice* has as its dual purpose to summarize some of the most significant findings of the social sciences in the area of race relations and, at the same time, to view those findings in the light of the values expressed in the theology, history, and tradition of Judaism.

May I suggest the use of the Opinionaire at the back of the book intended to help the reader examine more.closely his own attitudes. It was prepared with the cooperation of Professor Edward T. Hutchinson, Department of Sociology, University of Pennsylvania. So many have helped make this book possible. It was Rabbi Alexander Schindler, who, when he was director of the Commission on Education of the Union of American Hebrew Congregations, appreciated the need to demonstrate the relevance of Judaism to the major problems that plague mankind and so encouraged me in this effort. His successor, Rabbi Jack Spiro, equally committed to relevance in Jewish education, has given his full support to the idea of a text that can continue to evolve as new challenges confront us. I am, indeed, grateful to Rabbi Jacob Weinstein for valuable suggestions that stimulated my research into black and Jewish self-determination and to Rabbi Julius Kravetz, professor of rabbinics at the New York school of the Hebrew Union College-Jewish Institute of Religion for consultation in the intricacies of Jewish law. I am also grateful for the cooperation of James R. Cleaveland, U.S. Department of Labor and Professor Harry S. Broudy, Department of Education, University of Illinois. While these men should in no way be considered responsible for any of the shortcomings of this text, without their help, *Justice, Justice* simply would not have been written.

I also want to thank Ralph Davis, production manager of the UAHC whose cooperation made possible the publication and speedy revision of the book, and Robert Garvey, also of the UAHC, who publicized the text throughout the Jewish and general community. I am certainly grateful to Kivie Kaplan who so generously brought *Justice, Justice* to the attention of leaders in the black and white communities. I also appreciate the painstaking work of the UAHC's proofreading department. Finally, I wish to express my indebtedness to the following members of the Reading Committee of the Commission on Jewish Education: Mr. Marvin Braiterman, Rabbi Saul M. Diament, Rabbi Leon Fram, Mr. Max Frankel, Rabbi Bernard Kligfeld, Rabbi Leon Kronish.

It is my strong conviction that Jewish education should be concerned with exploring in more than a superficial fashion the great moral issues of our day. It is not enough for a teacher to depart from the text of Amos for a twenty-minute discussion of the poverty problem. Perhaps one day there will be in every Jewish school at least one course of study that brings knowledge needed for understanding the world, and values required for its redemption.

Henry Cohen

CONTENTS

Preface to Revised Edition
Section One: Of Rights and Wrongs
    Chapter One: A Way of Viewing   1
    Chapter Two: How Do You Answer a Revolution?   11
    Chapter Three: What Do You Really Believe about
                     Equality?   38 ✓
    Chapter Four: The Question of Responsibility   56
    Chapter Five: Into the Mainstream   82
Section Two: Allies or Adversaries?
    Chapter Six: Black Self-Determination and Jewish
                  Nationalism   115 ᵧ
    Chapter Seven: Community Control and the
                  Right to Power   131
    Chapter Eight: A New Look at Black Anti-
                  Semitism   143
Epilogue   167
Appendix I: Chronology of the Negro Revolt   169
Appendix II: On Civil Disobedience: Eight Alabama
                Clergymen and Martin Luther King   171
Appendix III: White and Nonwhite Education and
                Employment (Government Charts)   180
Appendix IV: White and Nonwhite Housing
                (Government Charts)   182
Appendix V: White and Nonwhite Families
                (Government Charts)   183
Appendix VI: Excerpts from the Official Summary of
                the Report of the President's National
                Advisory Commission on Civil Disorders   184
Bibliography   190
Notes   195
Opinionaire

SECTION ONE

Of Rights and Wrongs

Chapter One

A WAY OF VIEWING

Somewhere in Mississippi three young men were murdered because they had demanded freedom for the American Negro. Two were Jews. Somewhere in suburbia a congregant, on leaving the synagogue after the rabbi had preached a sermon on civil rights, whispered so everyone could hear: "Why should we worry about them? We have enough problems being Jewish! Besides, when we come to services, we want to hear something spiritual."

Deep into Dixie went hundreds of Jewish college students together with students of other faiths, in order to teach Negro children to read and encourage their parents to vote. In a city recently torn by riots, a successful businessman, speaking at an open forum, offered this advice: "Let the Negroes earn their rights, like we Jews did, by being responsible law-abiding citizens."

Members of a radical student organization, many of whom were Jewish, took over a university administration building to prevent the university from displacing black neighbors through its expansion program. In a Jewish neighborhood of the same city, the people booed the mayor claiming he had not taken a sufficiently strong hand against black anti-Semitism.

Within the Jewish community there are many ways of viewing the "Black Revolution." Some Jews are wholeheartedly committed to the call for equal rights. Others fear that Negroes want to go too far too fast. Still others view the racial tension by looking the other way. But is there a "Jewish view" of the "Black Revolution," not Jewish in the sense of representing the majority opinion of American Jews but in the sense of being implied by the ideals of Judaism? Can our religious heritage shed any light on such complex problems as discrimination, poverty, open housing, integration, race riots, and community control?

[1]

In this chapter we shall maintain that there is such a view, that it is motivated by a traditional concern with those social problems that cause human suffering, and that it requires us to bring together the understanding to be found in the social sciences and the values to be discovered in Judaism. This book is an attempt to help the reader achieve such a perspective, from which vantage point he will have to make his own moral decisions. But first, how can we be so sure that Judaism insists that we, as Jews, should be studying such a complicated social-legal-political-economic phenomenon as the "Black Revolution"?

1. The Relevance of Judaism

That Judaism has a three thousand year history of concern with specific problems that plague the community—this should be clear to anyone who has studied the Jewish heritage. In order to refresh our memory of this essential aspect of our faith, we would recall a few examples of this concern.

It was the prophet Amos who proclaimed that God despises ritual without righteousness. At what may have been a New Year celebration in the middle of the eighth century, B.C.E., the prophet suddenly appeared at the sanctuary in Beth-el and delivered perhaps the first Rosh Hashanah sermon. Amos did not speak in glittering generalities. Rather did he charge that certain economic policies ran counter to the Law of God: "Ye trample upon the poor and take from him exactions of wheat," that is, you are levying heavy taxes on those who can least afford to pay. He condemned the people for selling debtors into slavery and proclaimed: "Let justice well up as waters and righteousness as a mighty stream."[1]

During the rabbinic period, the ideals of biblical Judaism motivated much of Jewish law. The very purpose of that law was to bring the humane values of the Torah and the prophets into the social and economic institutions of the community. For example, in the Book of Leviticus, the farmer is commanded to leave a corner of his field for the needy. However, just how large a corner should be set aside remained an open question. A selfish farmer might decide to leave but a few ears of corn. So the Tannaim, whose decisions are recorded in the Mishnah, ruled that a minimum of one-sixtieth of the field should be allotted to the poor. How much more would depend upon the number of the poor and the size of the field.[2] Here is the modern concept of progressive taxation in a rabbinic statute that is two thousand years old!

We need not multiply quotations to make the point: Jewish tradition has never been content with merely advocating abstract ideals such as freedom and justice. Everyone will favor such generalities, for they can so easily be invoked to sanction the most blatant immorality. Obviously a religion that deals only in abstractions will soon be irrelevant to the real questions confronting mankind. Our tradition, however, insists on relevance. Our spiritual leaders have been in the midst of life. They have wrestled with the problems of poverty and prejudice, of property values and price control. To sum up: the prophets and the rabbis prevented Judaism from becoming a religion of pious platitudes.

2. The Universal Spirit of Judaism

There will always be those who say that Jews should direct their attention almost exclusively to the problems of the Jewish community, such as anti-Semitism. While we do care deeply about whatever affects the fate of the Jewish people, our faith insists that our hearts must be larger than ourselves.

During the Babylonian Exile, the prophet known as Deutero-Isaiah made quite clear that it was Israel's duty to do more than care for her own well being:

> . . . It is too light a thing that thou shouldest be My servant
> To raise up the tribes of Jacob.
> And to restore the offspring of Israel;

[3]

I will also give thee for a light of the nations,
That My salvation may be unto the end of the earth.[3]

As the servant of the Lord, Israel has a holy mission: "to make the right to go forth according to the truth," to be "a dimly burning wick" that will not be quenched "until the right is set forth in the earth."

In the same spirit, the rabbis asked: "Why in the commandment, *Tzedek, tzedek tirdof* (Justice, justice shalt thou pursue), is the word, *tzedek,* repeated? Why did not the Bible read simply: *Tzedek tirdof* (Justice shalt thou pursue)?" The answer: "To teach us that we must practice justice at all times, whether it be for our profit or for our loss, and towards all men, *towards Jews and non-Jews alike!*"[4]

Some centuries later, a chasidic *midrash* beautifully expressed the universal spirit of Judaism:

"Why," the student asked, "is the stork called *chasidah,* the loving one?"

"Because," the rabbi answered, "he gives so much love to his mate and to his young."

"Then why," asked the student, "if he gives such love to his mate and to his young, is the stork considered *trefe* (unclean) rather than *kosher?*"

"He is considered *trefe,*" the rabbi answered, "because *he gives love only to his own.*"[5]

As we shall learn in Chapter Three, there were times when the Jewish people, surrounded by an intensely hostile world, were less than loving towards their non-Jewish neighbors. It was perhaps natural that the Jew in the ghetto would think almost exclusively of his own problems. However, the essential moral commitment of Judaism has never been dependent upon how non-Jews feel about Jews, and that commitment requires: that we should pursue justice for Jew and non-Jew alike, that our love should not be limited to "our own."

3. A Moral Perspective

There are those who contend that since social problems

are political, economic or legal in nature, Judaism really has nothing to offer by way of solution. True, we cannot find in the Talmud those fiscal policies needed to alleviate poverty in an industrial state — but we can find in Jewish tradition a kind of moral perspective which can help us view these complex issues with a critical mind and a sensitive heart. As John Dewey has written: "Anything that obscures the fundamentally moral nature of the social problem is harmful."[6] But what does such a perspective involve?

a.   Facts and Consequences

Hillel stated that: "an ignorant man cannot be truly pious."[7] He was implying that knowledge is essential if one is to achieve the good life. *Talmud Torah* ("the study of law") was not a matter of reading pleasant stories each with its particular moral. *Talmud Torah* meant wrestling with the complex social and economic issues that confronted the community and striving to understand how the principles of the Bible and previous generations of rabbis could be applied to contemporary conditions. A good heart was not enough. So, today, if we are to achieve the good life, we too must struggle with the complexities of our time. If *Talmud Torah* is to have meaning in our generation, if we are to apply the ideals of our faith to the real world, then we had better strive for the deepest possible understanding of that world.

To gain a moral perspective on a particular problem, we might well begin by consulting those academic disciplines that bear upon the issue at hand. In the case of the "Black Revolution," these would include history, sociology, economics, psychology, and anthropology. Insights from such disciplines should help us answer questions ranging from the causes of poverty to the effects of racial isolation. In each area we should ask two questions: What are the facts? What would be the consequences of the possible courses of action?

It is not always easy to take the time for a calm appraisal of facts and consequences. For example, the riots which have been occurring with dismal regularity since 1964 may easily make some of us so indignant that we become incapable of understanding the causes of the violence. We

[5]

may even label any attempt at understanding to be "making excuses" for the rioters. And yet, if such human explosions are ever to cease, we will simply have to understand their causes. To be objective about such an emotional subject may well require a kind of spiritual effort. We will have to try to rise above our own impulsive feelings and to be biased only by the facts.

b.   How Your Neighbor Feels

To arrive at a just solution to any social conflict, each party should become acutely aware of how the other feels. For example, Negro parents should listen carefully to the fears expressed by white parents who do not want their children to attend classes in which a majority of the other students are from disadvantaged backgrounds. By the same token, white parents should imagine how it must feel to see their child's potential going to waste in crowded segregated demoralized schools.

This extremely difficult task—to identify with one's neighbor—is considered in our chasidic tradition to be the beginning of love. Rabbi Moshe Leib of Sassov declared to his disciples:

> I have learned how we must truly love our neighbor from a conversation between two villagers which I overheard.
> The first said: "Tell me, friend Ivan, do you love me?"
> The second: "I love you deeply."
> The first: "Do you know, my friend, what gives me pain?"
> The second: "How can I, pray, know what gives you pain?"
> The first: "If you do not know what gives me pain, how can you say that you truly love me?"[8]

A white man cannot possibly know exactly how it feels to be an American Negro. A remarkable attempt was made by John Howard Griffin, who darkened his skin and "passed" as a Negro in the South. Without taking such extreme measures, we can, at least, try to gain a deeper understanding of how it feels to be black in America.[9]

c.   Love and Justice

Having faced the facts, confronted the consequences, and become sensitive to the feelings of our fellowman—we then must face the "moral decision." Jewish tradition does not provide us with a rigid formula that can be applied to every situation and that is guaranteed to yield the ethically correct result. Instead, our faith offers us a remarkable collection of ideas and insights, laws and lore that *can* give us a sense of direction. One such insight was quoted above: To love your neighbor, you must understand what gives him pain. Perhaps the most familiar moral principle of the entire Torah is that great sentence in Leviticus considered by Rabbi Akiba as the highest ethical commandment: "Love thy neighbor as thyself."[10]

It has sometimes been alleged that Christianity is a religion based on love while Judaism is based on justice. This is an extremely misleading statement, since love and justice are inseparable one from the other. For Judaism, the principle of love raises questions of justice. For example, just what should the love of your neighbor require of you? To what extent should you sacrifice your own desires to meet his needs? (Should your family cancel its European vacation and donate the money to an anti-poverty agency?) Judaism, in the words of Rabbi Robert Gordis, has emphasized "the ethics of self-fulfillment," which regards it not only as natural and permissible but also as obligatory for every living organism to strive to maintain its life and function and to seek the maximum expression of its individuality, *so long as it does not vitiate or destroy the equal and similar right of other living creatures of the same order of being.*[11]

This is in marked contrast to the "ethics of self-abnegation" which demands total surrender of self-interest, as expressed in the words of Jesus: "If any man would go to law with thee, and take away thy coat, let him have thy cloak also," and "whosoever smiteth thee on thy right cheek, turn to him also the other."[12] While such an attitude was more strongly emphasized in Christianity than in Judaism, we do find this "altruistic" ideal expressed in the Mishnah as the definition of a Chasid: "What is mine is thine and what is thine is thine."[13] In contrast, the ethics of self-fulfillment is an almost literal interpretation of "love thy neighbor *as* thyself": your neighbor's needs should be considered just as important as (but not more important than) similar needs of your own.

The pursuit of justice is, then, an attempt to understand how we should balance our needs against those of our neighbors. Or, as Christian theologian Paul Tillich has suggested, justice is the form that love should take in society.[14] Should we follow the ethics of self-fulfillment, or should we try to be Chasidim, placing our neighbor's needs above our own? Finally, there is the profound question: Why should we —to any degree—give a care about our neighbor? Why not "play it cool" and remain aloof from people in trouble? With all the problems we face as individuals, who has the time, energy or inclination, really, to love his neighbor as himself?

This, then, is the kind of moral perspective our tradition seems to imply: (1) Facing the facts and confronting the consequences; (2) Becoming sensitive to how your neighbor feels; (3) Searching your soul to discover how you should balance your needs against those of your fellowman: in other words, exploring what love requires and justice demands.

4. The Problem of "Duplication"

The above section should provide an answer to the contention that in dealing with social issues, the synagogue is duplicating what is being done elsewhere in the community. The Jewish way of viewing is an attempt to bring together facts and values, to enable us not only to understand our world but to allow our faith to guide us in the building of a better world.

A less subtle answer to the argument that the synagogue may at times be doing what is already being done by other humanitarian groups is: Marvelous! We should rejoice in the so-called duplication, for in the field of ethical education, mankind has a long way to go, and we need all the help that is available. "The day is short, the task is great, and all who would labor for the master of the house are welcome."[15]

While we have discussed some of the reasons for Jewish concern with the "Black Revolution" and have suggested a Jewish way of viewing it, we have not even touched upon many other questions that revolve around the issue: How far should the synagogue go into the social arena?

Should a social action committee urge congregants to support: (1) a civil rights bill that would enforce open occupancy; (2) greater expenditures for the war against poverty; (3) a local school bond issue? Should the rabbi take stands on such questions from the pulpit? Should a rabbi take part in demonstrations which advocate programs opposed by most members of his congregation?

Should a synagogue sponsor a nursery school for disadvantaged children or should such projects be left to public agencies? Most American Jewish organizations favor a high wall of separation between church and state. Can one reconcile this view with the active concern of Jewish religious groups with issues ranging from U.S. relations with Communist China to American foreign policy in the Middle East?

What to Expect

In the chapters to come the development of the "Black Revolution" will be traced, from the Civil Rights movement to the current cry for self-determination and community control. Then several fundamental philosophic questions will be raised: What are the meanings of such terms as "equality" and "human rights"? Why should one give a care about his neighbor's rights? How should conflicts between rights be resolved? The sensitive issue of who or what is really responsible for the high proportion of poor in the black community will be discussed, as will be the major proposals that have been made as a means of bringing more Negroes into the mainstream of American life.

The latter section of the book, titled "Allies or Adversaries?" will deal with the highly charged issues that have emerged from the conflict between blacks who claim the right to self-determination and Jews some of whom feel threatened by the new thrust in the black community. The ideology of black self-determination will be compared with various forms of Jewish nationalism, the pros and cons of community control will be argued, and the phenomenon of black anti-Semitism will be carefully examined.

This Jewish view of the "Black Revolution" will not provide simple formulas for the solving of all racial tension. It will perhaps make possible a deeper understanding of the crisis as well as a fresh awareness of the relevance of Judaism to the real problems that plague mankind. There is one certainty. Judaism does not allow us the luxury of indifference. In the words of the Talmud:

> If the community is in trouble, a man must not say, "I will go to my house, and eat and drink, and peace shall be with thee, O my soul." But a man must share in the troubles of the community, even as Moses did. He who shares in its troubles is worthy to see its consolation.[16]

Our community is in trouble. May we be worthy to see its consolation.*

---

*Before continuing with the following chapters, the reader may wish to complete the Opinionaire, at the end of the book.

Dr. Martin Luther King (center) leads the Civil Rights
demonstrators on the last leg of their Selma to Montgomery
march. With Dr. King are Dr. Ralph Bunche (4th from left)
and Rev. Ralph Abernathy (2nd from left). March, 1965.
Dr. King was assassinated in Memphis, Tenn., on April 4,
1968. UPI Photo.

Civil Rights demonstrators kneel in prayer on steps of the county courthouse after a protest march in Natchez, Miss., October, 1965. UPI Photo.

"Project Free" demands open housing in Bryn Mawr, Pa., December, 1967. Courtesy, Theodore Hetzel and Philadelphia Tribune.

Children of poverty, Belzoni, Miss., June, 1967. UPI Photo.

Resident of "Lightning," slum area near downtown Atlanta, chops down a fence to use as firewood. UPI Photo.

Rats hiding behind a tenement wall. UPI Photo.

The danger of fire is greater in the slum. From this third floor window a man jumped to escape a blaze. Philadelphia, 1965. Courtesy, Philadelphia Tribune.

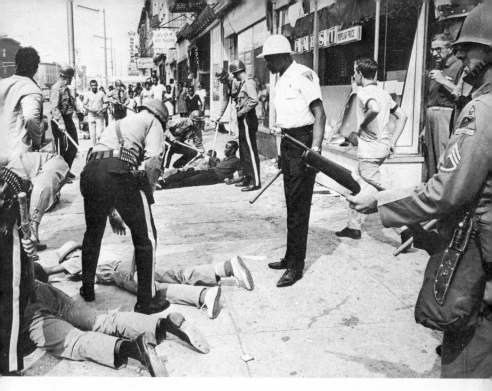

National guardsmen and state police detain looters in
Newark following the July, 1967 riot in New Jersey's
largest city. UPI Photo.

Riot damage, Detroit, 1967. AP Photo, Courtesy, Philadelphia Tribune.

Chapter Two

HOW DO YOU ANSWER A REVOLUTION?

On December 1, 1955, Mrs. Rosa Parks was seated in the "colored" section of a crowded bus in Montgomery, Alabama. The driver ordered her to stand so that a white man could sit. Quietly she refused, and quickly she was arrested. Her simple assertion of human dignity gave to the Negroes of Montgomery the courage to boycott the city's buses for an entire year. Singing "my feet is tired but my soul is rested," they walked. Under the leadership of Rev. Martin Luther King, Jr. they won. Some would say that was how the "Black Revolution" began.

In this chapter after examining the early stages of the revolt, we shall follow the struggle as it moves from the south to the north. We shall see the demand for freedom from discrimination by the state and individuals become transformed into a demand for freedom from oppressive social and economic conditions. We shall then consider the response to the frustration of hopes unfulfilled that has taken the form of the movement towards self-determination and community control. From time to time the narrative will be broken in order to discuss the strategies and philosophies of Negro leaders in the light of Jewish values and experiences.

The Seeds of Revolt

Historians may never agree on exactly when the "Black Revolution" began. Some might say that the Second World War set it off. In 1941, after A. Philip Randolph threatened a march on Washington, President Franklin D. Roosevelt banned discrimination in the country's defense industries. Labor unions were still segregated, but many young Negroes in their own "locals" learned methods of political organization which they would later employ in their drive for civil rights. Negro veterans, returning to their homes, could hardly be expected to tolerate second-class citizenship in the land they had risked their lives to defend.

One might contend that the opening salvo of the revolt was fired by the United States Supreme Court when, on May 17, 1954, the court rendered its opinion in the case of Brown versus the Board of Education of Topeka. After hearing the arguments advanced by Thurgood Marshall of the NAACP, the court ruled that compulsory segregation in state-supported elementary and secondary schools violated the clause in the Fourteenth Amendment which states that all born or naturalized citizens should be afforded "equal protection of the laws." No longer could "separate but equal" facilities be considered truly equal; therefore the southern school system found itself in violation of the law of the land.

The court's ruling was widely hailed by proponents of equal rights for all Americans. However, ten years after the decision, only token integration had taken place in the South. In 1964, the percentage of Negro children in school with whites ranged from .02 percent in Mississippi to 7.26 percent in Texas. Thousands of Southern Negroes wondered what good is the legal process if it can bring no changes into their lives. The hopes raised by the court ruling were not fulfilled, and the resulting disillusion added fuel to the fire of Negro discontent.

The Revolt Is Born

For Louis Lomax, author of *The Negro Revolt*, the Montgomery bus boycott of 1955-6 was the real beginning.[1] For the first time in the South, the Negroes of an entire community arose *en masse* to demand respect for their human rights. However, the boycott, by itself, did not achieve the victory. Buses were not desegregated until the Supreme Court ruled that the laws requiring segregation in

Alabama's buses were unconstitutional. The Montgomery boycott could be considered the beginning perhaps because *it was this combination of mass demonstration and governmental action that was to provide the dynamic power behind at least the civil rights phase of the revolt.*

But the movement, once begun, sputtered. It was not until 1960—four years after the boycott—that the Southern Negro decided to take another "stride towards freedom." In 1957, Congress did pass a mild civil rights bill (the first in 82 years), and President Eisenhower dispatched troops to Little Rock so that nine Negro children might enter Central High School. In 1959, the Supreme Court declared unconstitutional the "massive resistance" of Virginia districts which had attempted to close the entire public school system and set up private schools for whites only. Still, during the four years after Montgomery, the Negroes of the South remained apparently passive. But why? Evidently slavery and the Jim Crow System had so crushed the spirit of their victims that almost a century after the Civil War, they were still reluctant to struggle for their freedom. This may be history's most severe indictment of "White Supremacy": that the system so dehumanized the Southern Negro that for generations he was incapable of demanding equal rights. As Rabbi Hanokh, an eighteenth-century Chasid, remarked about another oppression: "The real exile of Israel in Egypt was that they had learned to endure it."[2]

In February, 1960, a seventeen-year-old student, McNeil Joseph, attending an all-Negro college in Greensboro, North Carolina, rebelled against the apathy of his elders. He, and three friends, "sat-in" at the lunch counter of Woolworth's and 1960 became the year of the "sit-in." Thousands of whites and Negroes in a hundred Southern cities parked themselves at the counters of stores that allowed Negroes to buy anything they wanted except food. After several months of such protests, chain store executives announced the desegregation of lunch counters in scores of Southern cities. The students who sparked the sit-in movement had learned they did not have to wait for the established Negro leadership to plead their cases in the courts. They had discovered that nonviolent direct action could be an effective technique, so they formed SNCC, the Student Nonviolent Coordinating Committee.

Using nonviolent action to promote social change was not a new idea. CORE, the Congress of Racial Equality, had been founded in 1942, on this Gandhian principle. However, it was not until the spring of 1961 that CORE, under the leadership of its new director, James Farmer, put the technique to use on a large scale. Scores of "Freedom Riders" climbed into buses and headed South in order to desegregate interstate bus terminals. In Alabama, riders were beaten in Anniston, Birmingham, and Montgomery, where federal marshals and the national guard were called out to restrain the white mob. During the summer a few terminals were desegregated, and in the fall a ruling of the Interstate Commerce Commission effectively put an end to all segregation in interstate facilities.

In September, 1962, James Meredith entered the University of Mississippi, despite the resistance of Governor Barnett. There followed a night of horror on the Oxford campus, as 2,500 whites charged federal marshals. Two men were killed and 375 injured before order was restored by regular army troops brought in from Memphis.

1963: Turning Point in Birmingham

In January, 1963, one hundred years after the signing of the Emancipation Proclamation, Protestant, Catholic, and Jewish leaders gathered in Chicago for the first National Conference on Religion and Race. Rabbi Balfour Brickner reported that the delegates were extremely critical of the failure of both churches and synagogues to demonstrate their concern, to denounce racial injustice and to encourage cooperative programs that would combat racial discrimination.

However, it remained for the events in Birmingham, 1963, to shame the conscience of America and to shake the apathy of the Negro poor. Rev. King, director of the Southern

Christian Leadership Conference, and Rev. Fred Shuttelsworth presented Mayor Boutwell with a package of demands, ranging from desegregation of lunch counters to the upgrading and hiring of Negroes without discrimination by local employers. When the demands were not met, there followed weeks of demonstrations, during which Rev. King ignored a court injunction banning further marches, and was consequently imprisoned. On April 16, from his jail cell he wrote to his clergy critics an eloquent letter in defense of civil disobedience. Sheriff Bull Conner's use of police dogs to halt the marchers shocked the nation and perhaps helped move Birmingham's civic leaders to end the tragic conflict by coming to terms with the demonstrators.

While significant steps were taken to meet the demands of the Negro community, the white extremists were not willing to give in so easily. The home of Rev. A. D. King, brother of Martin, was bombed and young Negroes staged a riot in retaliation. The mood of violence spread to Jackson, Mississippi, where in June, Medgar Evers, of the local NAACP, was fatally shot in the back. That fall in Birmingham, four little girls were in Sunday school learning to love their neighbors when a bomb was thrown into the church. The little girls were killed—and Rev. King bitterly remembers—at the funeral "no white faces could be seen save for a pathetically few courageous ministers."[3]

Birmingham was a major turning-point in the history of the "Black Revolution." The rage of the Negro, so long masked behind the servant's smile, came to the surface for all to see. Most important, for the first time, the Negro poor became part of the protest movement.[4] As far north as Chicago, the mood of Birmingham caught hold of the inhabitants of "Bronzeville," and Mayor Daly was so harassed by sit-ins, school boycotts, and picketing that he forced a reluctant city council to pass an open housing law.

Let us pause in our narrative to consider one of the most controversial techniques used in the "Black Revolution," that of civil disobedience, as practiced by Rev. King and as defended by him in his letter from the Birmingham jail. In that letter he wrote that one is morally bound to disobey an unjust law.

Critics of this philosophy have argued that if everyone were to set himself up as a judge to determine which law is just and which, unjust, the result would be anarchy. Rev. King has replied in effect that the just quality of a law depends not on the whim of the individual but on objective criteria. For example, if the law is degrading to human personality or if the victims had no part in making it, then such a law would not be just. Such justified disobedience has an honorable tradition from Shadrach, Meshach, and Abed-nego in Daniel to Mahatma Gandhi.

We would add that the medieval philosopher, Moses Maimonides, held that Jewish law clearly allowed for civil disobedience under certain conditions:

> He who disobeys a king's mandate, because he is engaged in the performance of one *mitzvah* or another, even an insignificant one, is relieved of guilt. . . and one need not add that if the mandate itself involves the violation of one of God's mandates, it need not be obeyed! [5]

Perhaps the earliest instance of the tradition of civil disobedience was that of the Hebrew midwives who ignored the command of the Pharaoh and saved the male children of the Israelites. The rabbis commented that their actions were praiseworthy because the law was discriminatory, affecting only Jewish males, and therefore should not have been obeyed.[6]

Discussion: Before exploring the pros and cons of civil disobedience read, in Appendix I, a letter from eight Alabama clergymen to Rev.

King and excerpts from his reply.

It is often said that the encouragement of nonviolent disobedience may well lead to violent lawlessness. When this does happen, who is primarily responsible for the violence?—the nonviolent demonstrator?—the person (white or Negro) who is violent?—the community that allows injustice? Do you think there is a moral difference between one who breaks the law for gain and tries to escape punishment and one who breaks only a law he considers unjust and is willing to accept punishment in order to call attention to the injustice?

If you support Dr. King, how would you answer the charge that any individual can set up his own criteria for what is a just law and so disobedience must lead to disrespect for all law?

If you oppose Dr. King, how would you justify the Boston Tea Party and the American Revolution?*

The Civil Rights Law of 1964

In August, 1963, A. Philip Randolph and Bayard Rustin led 210,000 whites and Negroes in a march on Washington, in order to urge Congress to pass President Kennedy's Civil Rights Bill. The President was not to see the bill's passage. Less than three months after the march, America was stunned by the unbelievable tragedy that happened in Dallas. It was left to President Lyndon Johnson to carry on the struggle for the legislation. In June he signed the Civil Rights Act of 1964, which represented the first large-scale effort of Congress to apply the "equal protection" clause of the Fourteenth Amendment to race relations. Discrimination on the basis of race, color, religion or national origin in hotels, motels, restaurants, lunch counters, movie houses . . . and other places of public accommodation was prohibited, as was segregation of such public facilities as parks, libraries, and hospitals. Employers, labor unions, and employment agencies were required to treat all persons without regard to race, color, religion, national origin or sex. This section would, by 1968, apply to employers and unions with 25 workers. School desegregation was encouraged, and the U.S. Department of Justice and the federal courts were given powers to

---

*See Opinionaire Item 6.

deal with violations of this act and other civil rights policies.

The role of organized religion in promoting the passage of the 1964 bill was widely recognized, and the Jewish community played its part with distinction. At the National Conference on Religion and Race, Rabbi Abraham Heschel had made it clear that when we segregate our fellowman, we segregate God. Two days before the Senate was to vote on the bill, sixteen rabbis and the director of their Commission on Social Action of Reform Judaism, Mr. Al Vorspan, flew to St. Augustine, Florida, to participate in demonstrations against segregation in that community.[7] Arrested while attempting to desegregate Monson's Motor Lodge, they spent the night crowded in a tiny jail cell intended for six. In a letter explaining why they came to St. Augustine, the rabbis wrote:

> . . . We came because we could not stand silently by our brother's blood. We had done that too many times before. We have been vocal in our exhortation of others but the idleness of our hands too often revealed an inner silence . . . We came as Jews who remember the millions of faceless people who stood quietly, watching the smoke rise from Hitler's crematoria. We came because we know that second only to silence, the greatest danger to man is loss of faith in man's capacity to act.[8]

This was but one incident among hundreds in which religiously motivated white Americans, by their actions, created the moral climate so that the passage of the landmark bill was assured. As one influential senator remarked: "There is nothing more powerful than an idea whose time has come."

The COFO Summer

Once the 1964 Civil Rights Act was signed, the revolution moved to assure Negroes of the right to vote. Because of unfair testing procedures and intimidation, only 23 percent of eligible Negroes were registered in Alabama and as few as 6.7 percent in Mississippi. So, in the summer of 1964, COFO

(The Council of Federated Organizations: CORE, SNCC, SCLC, NAACP) recruited 1,200 volunteers, most of them from college campuses, to go to Mississippi to encourage voter registration and also to set up community centers and establish "Freedom Schools" where children could be taught courses ranging from remedial reading to political science. There was a price: Andrew Goodman, James Chaney, and Michael Schwerner were brutally murdered.

According to the FBI at least 50 persons had been involved in a conspiracy to murder Schwerner, a young Jew from Brooklyn who had been in Mississippi for about six months with his wife and had opened CORE's community center in Meridian. Leaders of the White Knights of the Ku Klux Klan were convinced that he was the ring-leader of the invading "Yankee beatniks, Jews, and other scum."[9] Goodman, another Jew, and Chaney, a Negro, were killed because they happened to be with Schwerner when he went to the small town of Philadelphia to investigate a church-burning. For months after the murder, anti-Semitic handbills were posted on the bulletin board of the courthouse in Philadelphia. One read: "Jew-Communists Behind Race-Mixing."

There were no more racist murders that summer in Mississippi but one of COFO's counselling clergy, Rabbi Arthur Lelyveld of Cleveland, was severely beaten in Hattiesburg. The involvement of a significant number of Jews from the North in such mass efforts to change certain political traditions of the Deep South was an undeniable fact. Estimates of the proportion of Jewish college students among the COFO volunteers range widely from one-fifth to one-half.[10] Whatever their number, they were often bitterly resented by Jews living in the South. It was feared that these intruders would stir up anti-Semitism which would be directed not against the "foreigners" who could go back to New York but against the local Jewish citizens, most of whom were business or professional people, dependent for their livelihood on the goodwill of the non-Jewish community.

Discussion: Do you believe the Jewish college students had a right to work with the "freedom movement" in Mississippi? If your answer is affirmative, how would you have answered a Jewish merchant from Jackson, who claimed that you were fomenting anti-Semitism? If your answer is negative, how would you reconcile such a condemnation of these students with the moral imperative of Judaism, "Justice, justice shalt thou pursue"? There is a close connection between anti-Negro and anti-Jewish feeling among Southern bigots. What might this connection imply to Jews worried about anti-Semitism? How do you think you would feel if you were a Southern Jewish merchant?

The Voting Rights Act of 1965

In March, 1965, 525 Negroes tried to march from Selma to Montgomery, Alabama, to petition for the right to vote. They were turned back by state troopers and Sheriff Jim Clark's possemen, who waded into the marchers with whips, clubs, and tear gas. Rev. King called for help from the nation's clergy. One who responded, Rev. James J. Reeb, a Unitarian minister, was killed, when he and two other clergymen were beaten by a gang of bigots. In early April, 300 men and women marched all the way from Selma to Montgomery, and 25,000 gathered at the state capitol. Thus, what was perhaps the climax of the campaign to achieve equality under the law took place where the revolution had begun with a boycott almost ten years before.

There was another life to be given in the cause of freedom. After the march Mrs. Viola Liuzzo, while driving down the highway to Selma, was shot at the wheel of her car. She left behind a six-year-old daughter who wondered, "Why couldn't Mommy have died just from being old?"

In August, 1965, the Voting Rights Act was passed. At long last, literacy and other tests could no longer be used, as they had been for nearly a century, to disenfranchise Negroes. Federal examiners could go to any state or district, suspend discriminatory tests and actually conduct the registration. A sixth grade education was considered an indication of literacy, and intimidation aimed at preventing a person from voting became a federal offense. Such provisions led to significant increases in Negro voting. This law together with the Civil Rights Act of 1964 were the major legislative achievements of the first phase of the "Black Revolution." However, for Negroes living in rural poverty or urban slums, there was still a very long way to go.

The Demand for Real Equality

In a perceptive analysis, published in the February, 1965, issue of *Commentary,* Bayard Rustin wrote that "the legal foundations of racism in America (have been) destroyed": No longer could any governmental body deny the Negro the right to vote, or to attend schools with whites, or enforce segregation in places of public accommodations. Rustin continued: The Civil Rights movement "is now concerned not merely with removing the barriers to full *opportunity* but with achieving the *fact of equality.*"11 While individual employers may be required to offer qualified Negroes job opportunities, what can be done about the thousands who are not sufficiently skilled, because their capacities have never been allowed to develop fully? They want to be equal in fact, not in theory. So the barriers today are not so much individual or governmental acts which might be made illegal by legislation. Rather are they those conditions found primarily in our city slums that make it impossible for the Negro to take his place in the mainstream of American life.

Consequently, the revolution has come to be focused *less on equality before the law and more on social and economic equality, less on banning the discriminatory acts of individuals and more on attacking the basic causes of ignorance and poverty, less on the South as a region and more on America as a nation.*

It was in the streets and tenements of the great Northern cities that the revolution for real equality caught fire. From 1940 to 1963, 3.3 million Negroes moved from the South to other sections of the country. In 1964, while slightly over half the Negroes still lived in the South, the first six cities in Negro population were New York, Chicago,

Philadelphia, Detroit, Washington (a border city), and Los Angeles.[12] These hundreds of thousands of non-Southern Negroes had not been materially affected by the revolution. They could already ride in the front of the bus, have coffee at Woolworth's and register to vote. Theirs was the overwhelming problem of what Kenneth Clark has called "the dark ghetto."

The grievances of the Negro slumdweller should be familiar to all Americans: overcrowding, inferior schools, police brutality, exploitation by merchants and landlords, and, above all, unemployment. In Chapter Four we shall look closely at the conditions in the ghetto and attempt to understand their causes. For the purpose of this brief history, it is enough to recognize that ten years after the Montgomery boycott, for thousands of Negroes, life in the ghetto *had not significantly improved.* The national unemployment rate for Negroes had remained, since 1954, at least twice as high as the rate for whites.[13] Of tremendous importance is the fact that the jobless rate among Negro youth (age 14-19) had *increased* from 13.5 in 1955 to 22.6 in 1965![14] In 1964, in Harlem, 23.3 percent of the teenagers were out of school and out of a job. In the Watts area of Los Angeles, just prior to the riot, the corresponding figure was 33 percent.[15]

So despite the legislative victories for civil rights, the slumdweller was at least as miserable as he was before the bus boycott of 1954. Little wonder that the dark ghetto became the center of the second phase of the revolt: *the demand for real equality.*

The Frustrated Revolution

The "northern-urban" phase of the "Black Revolution" may be traced back to 1961, when TWO (The Woodlawn Organization) was formed on the South Side of Chicago by Saul Alinsky, director of the Industrial Arts Foundation. Alinsky's purpose was to enable the slumdwellers to form an effective political organization in which the poor themselves—not welfare workers or city officials—would decide what they needed and how their needs should be met. TWO was sufficiently effective to force the adoption of a code of ethics by the local merchants and to prevent the University of Chicago from carrying out a building program that, according to TWO, "would have been detrimental to the neighborhood." However, as has been noted, it was only in 1963, after Birmingham, that Northern Negroes in large numbers joined the revolution.[16]

In February, 1964, 464,000 students stayed out of the public schools of New York as a protest against the high degree of racial isolation in the school system. During the same year, to achieve integration, demonstrations or boycotts were carried out in Boston, Buffalo, Cincinnati, Cleveland, Kansas City, Chicago, Gary, Indiana, and Chester, Pennsylvania. However, these tactics did not achieve their goals. They did provoke angry white parents to form organizations that would vigorously oppose any policy aimed at encouraging integration.

Shortly after the passage of the Civil Rights Act of 1964—a major triumph of the legal phase of the revolt— "the Social Dynamite," that James Conant warned was accumulating in our large cities, exploded.[17] Riots broke out in Harlem, Brooklyn, and Rochester, New York; Elizabeth and Paterson, New Jersey; and Philadelphia, Pennsylvania. The slum Negro was striking blindly at the white world that would not let him in. The loss to white merchants from burning and looting ran into the millions of dollars, but it was generally Negroes who were injured and killed and the Negro community that lay in ruins.

On August 20, 1964, President Johnson signed the Economic Opportunity Act, popularly known as the "War Against Poverty." Under the leadership of Sargent Shriver, the federal government developed such programs as Head Start (two months of pre-school preparation for poor children), the Job Corps (remedial educational and vocational training for dropouts), the Neighborhood Youth Corps (community service work for the neighborhood unemployed), and VISTA (a domestic Peace Corps). Most controversial were the federal grants made available to local community action organizations for grass-roots assistance to low income families in employment.[18] However, for the slum Negro these programs were too little and too late.

The following summer in the Watts area of Los Angeles, two weeks after the passage of the Voting Rights Act of 1965, what happened was not a riot but an insurrection. Nearly one thousand business establishments were totally or partially destroyed, and property damage rose to 35 million dollars. 4,000 were arrested, 900 were injured, and 34 people were killed. 29 of those who died were Negroes, most of them shot by police in the effort to restore order.

Ever since Watts, the midsummer riot has come to be feared as an annual event. In 1966, the major explosions took place in Chicago and Cleveland, but the summer of 1967 proved to be more lethal than any that had preceded. The mood was set by outbreaks in Cincinnati, Atlanta, and Buffalo. Then came Newark where 23 were killed. Rocks were thrown and stores looted in more than a score of cities throughout the country. It was, however, in Detroit that violence reached a crescendo and shattered a proud city, considered to have one of the better poverty programs in the nation. There, 11,500 federal troops and national guardsmen, supported by tanks, fought a guerilla war against snipers firing from tenements. During the day, looters went about as though they were at a carnival, but when the damage was reckoned, 43 persons had lost their lives, 35 of them, Negro; more than 1,000 had been injured, 5,000 arrested, and property loss was estimated at more than 48 million dollars. Even Watts had been "surpassed."

By the mid-sixties the "Black Revolution" could accurately be called the "frustrated revolution." The war in Vietnam, which had developed by 1967 into a major conflict involving more than 500,000 Americans, became the issue of first priority in the nation's mind and budget. Anti-poverty agencies, instead of being able to expand their programs, often found their funds reduced. The war against poverty turned out to be only a skirmish. Some whites defended the cuts by pointing out that the unemployment rate among non-whites in 1968 was "only" 6.7 percent, down from 10 percent in 1960.[19] However, in 1959, 25 percent of the blacks were living in poverty and by 1966, according to the Social Security Administration, the proportion was 33 percent. Among the reasons for a lower unemployment rate and a higher incidence of poverty were: (1) the proportionately larger number of children in the ghetto and (2) the rising cost of living. Another major indicator of frustration was the high proportion of the "sub-employed": those out of work and those working part-time at menial jobs. According to the Department of Labor, the sub-employment rate in November, 1966, ranged from 30 percent in the New York ghettos to 50 percent in New Orleans. Finally there were and still are a large number of blacks never discovered by the census-takers in slum areas: in 1967, the Department of Labor found an "undercount" of 20 percent. As Michael Harrington has written: "This means that there are several million Americans whose conditions of life are so mercurial that they do not even qualify to be a statistic."[20]

On the political scene there were occasional rays of hope. Among Negroes elected or appointed to high office were, in 1966, Senator Edward Brooks of Massachusetts; in 1967, John Stokes and Richard Hatcher, mayors of Cleveland, Ohio, and Gary, Indiana respectively; also in 1967, Thurgood Marshall, associate justice of the Supreme Court; in 1969, Charles Evers, mayor of Fayette, Mississippi. However, also in 1969, Thomas Bradley was defeated in his effort to become mayor of Los Angeles, because of the anti-black sentiment in that city.

In general, the mood of the late 1960's was one of bitter disillusion, the greatest single moment of anguish coming early in April, 1968. Martin Luther King was in Memphis, planning a march on behalf of the city's sanitation workers to demonstrate that the black man could still protest effectively in a nonviolent manner. He had been looking forward to leading a Poor People's March on Washington later that month, but he was not destined to do so. On the evening of April 4, Rev. King was fatally shot, and America was shocked into shame.

Never before in the nation's history had the death of a private citizen so shaken the conscience of white America. Vice-president Humphrey together with governors, senators, and foreign dignitaries went to Atlanta for the funeral. On April 10, the House of Representatives passed a civil rights bill that would by 1970 strike down discriminatory racial barriers in about 80 percent of the nation's housing. The law would not apply to private single dwellings sold or rented by the owner without the services of an agent. The bill had previously passed the Senate but faced possibly crippling amendments in the House. Shaken by Rev. King's death, the House took action, thus sending the legislation to the President for his signature.

The assassination had, however, more ominous consequences. During the week after the murder, there were incidents of racial violence in at least 110 cities. Although in most areas, the damage was minor by past standards, in twelve cities, including Chicago, Washington, D.C., Baltimore, and Kansas City, the burning and looting required the presence of federal troops, or national guardsmen, and 39 lives were lost. To some of the more militant young blacks, Rev. King's death was a symbol of the failure of nonviolence. They would argue that the most recent civil rights bill was passed—as was most other such legislation—not out of shame or compassion but out of fear. They would continue to claim that the only way to bring about fundamental change is to frighten the "power structure" into significant action by the threat or use of violence.

Discussion: Violence and the White Backlash

What is your view of the above argument in favor of the threat or use of violence? Do the riots cause "white backlash"? If so, how does this backlash affect the chances of anti-poverty legislation? How would you respond to a young Negro who argued that anti-poverty programs were established only *after* the riots; therefore, violence is justified? When, if ever, is violence justified as a means of righting social wrongs?

When Richard Nixon, running on a platform of "law and order," was elected president in 1968, some blacks (and whites) pointed to his victory as proof that the majority of Americans are unwilling to deal with the causes of social unrest and are content to try to suppress the symptoms. The new President's proposal to extend the Voting Rights Act in a form more palatable to the South was greeted with cries of indignation by civil rights leaders. However, at this writing, it is too soon to evaluate the efforts of the Nixon administration. The most crucial questions are still very open: Can the President end the war in Vietnam? Should the war be terminated, would a high proportion of the resources being poured into it be channelled into a truly effective war on poverty in America? Some disillusioned blacks have come to feel that no administration within the present social system will respond adequately to the needs of their community. So, they have developed a new movement that is posing a challenge to all Americans.

Black Power and Self-Determination

1. The New Ideology

By the mid-sixties many black leaders had come to feel that the strategies effectively employed in the first phase of the revolt were no longer useful. A sit-in might help open a restaurant to customers regardless of race but it could hardly produce jobs, housing, and education. Some of the younger voices charged that the established civil rights leadership with its emphasis on painfully slow legal procedures, its nonviolent demonstrations and its close association with white liberals, was unable to bring about the kind of fundamental changes demanded by the slum dweller.

These voices raised the cry of "Black Power," a term that has been applied to diverse strategies ranging from bloc voting for a black mayor to the advocacy of paramilitary training for black youths for purposes of self-defense. Despite the variety of interpretations of "Black Power," four ideas have generally been associated with its program and philosophy:

a. Pride: Blacks (the term, Negro, is considered the white man's creation originally used by him to cut the black man's tie to his African origin) should have greater pride in their own race.

b. Separatism: Blacks should depend not on the white world but on their own political and economic power to achieve their ends. Alliances with white liberals inhibit the revolution, so let them work in their own community and let blacks guide their own struggle for liberation. Integration into today's white society with its false values is not desirable.

c. Radicalism: The solution to the black man's problem can not be found in the white world as it now exists. Therefore, fundamental changes must take place in the present political, economic and social system.

d. Self-determination: There should be black control of those institutions that affect the lives of black people: e.g., the schools, businesses, health, welfare, and law enforcement agencies that serve the ghetto.

To implement these ideas, a black power conference in Newark, in July, 1967, advocated a set of specific programs, among them: a black university with subsidiary colleges in each city, a black national holiday honoring such heroes as Malcolm X, a school for black political organization, the establishment of financial institutions (banks, loan offices) controlled by blacks, massive refusal of blacks to fight in Vietnam. This opposition to participation in the Vietnam War reflected the view that blacks should not fight against Asians who are engaged in their own struggle for national liberation.

In the popular mind, "Black Power" has been widely associated with the threat and use of violence. The riots were viewed by SNCC leader H. Rap Brown as the first stage of a rebellion that would eventually force the basic changes needed in the society. The new mood of the formerly nonviolent SNCC was made clear when, after the Detroit explosion of 1967, Brown threatened: "We built this country up and we can tear it down."[21] In June, 1969, George Murray, Black Panthers' minister of education was quoted as threatening the destruction of factories and airports and the assassination of white officials in retaliation for the black lives they have taken. Because of the widespread publicity given such statements, it is not generally realized that most of the advocates of "Black Power" reject violent revolution as a futile tactic and favor instead the development of political, economic and consumer power by means of black community organization.

The ideas loosely associated with "Black Power" have recently become more clearly articulated in an ideology characterized by its programmatic emphasis on black self-determination: The white society is not willing to integrate black people into its way of life, so who needs the corrupt materialistic world of the white man! Let the black man develop his own culture and community and through local control determine his own future.

The most popular hero among self-determinists is Malcolm X, who, while serving a prison sentence, was converted to the Muslim religious nationalism of Elijah Muhammad. As a Muslim, Malcolm began to take great pride in himself and his race. Eventually he became disillusioned with the movement when he learned more about the personal life of Elijah Muhammad. Psychologically emancipated from his "master," he journeyed to Mecca and returned having rejected the Muslim doctrines of white inferiority and strict separatism and prepared, without relinquishing his black pride, to work with those whites who understood the black man's struggle. However, Malcolm was assassinated, probably on the orders of Elijah, himself, before he was able effectively to put his new ideas into practice.

The philosophy and program of black self-determination has been advocated by Stokely Carmichael, Charles Hamilton, Harold Cruse, and Eldridge Cleaver, among others. Their views are discussed in Chapter Six, which compares and contrasts black self-determination with the various expressions of Jewish nationalism in the late nineteenth and early twentieth century. For purposes of this historic survey, it is sufficient to comment briefly on the response of the black community to this new ideology.

2. Self-Determination within the Black Community

There are no easy ways of accurately discovering how blacks are reacting to the new ideology: the community mood changes from year to year and individual attitudes vary depending on which aspect of the ideology is being considered. Since 1964, when—according to an impressive study made by Professor Gary Marx—black nationalism had little support, the young self-determinists seem to have assembled a significant following.[22] Although this group, by its own admission is still a distinct minority among blacks, it does wield increasing influence.

Black leaders of the more established organizations have given support to certain aspects of black self-determination. Speaking to a CORE convention in July, 1968, Whitney Young, Jr., director of the Urban League, said that:

> ... [he] wanted to make it clear that the Urban League believes strongly in that interpretation of "Black Power" that emphasizes self-determination, pride, self-respect, participation and control of one's destiny and community affairs. [23]

It is worth noting that Young did *not* endorse the separatist concept that cooperation with white liberals is futile, nor did he support the radical doctrine that instead of reform there must be a fundamental change of the social and economic system. Roy Wilkins, director of the NAACP, has also stated that the use of political power by blacks is not a new idea. His organization, without taking a stand on community control, continues its efforts by working for equal rights through Congress and the courts.

CORE, though apparently split as to whether blacks should try to work within the system, has endorsed self-determination, and its director, Roy Innis, has attempted to influence government leaders to make possible more local control. SNCC, fragmented by personal and ideological conflicts, is no longer a truly national organization. It has been replaced in some areas by the Black Panthers who strongly endorse the self-determinist position. The SCLC, under Rev. Ralph Abernathy, has fared poorly since the failure of Resurrection City in the summer of 1968. Set up as the climax of the Poor People's March, poorly organized and mired in mud, the city did not arouse the national conscience and the SCLC was billed $71,795 by the government for the cost of tearing it down. Still trying to apply the technique of nonviolent protest marches to the problems of the sixties, the SCLC is considered out-of-touch by many self-determinists. Among newer leaders, George Wiley, director of the National Welfare Rights Organization, supported by some thirty thousand mothers on welfare, has pushed for more government assistance and has avoided ideological stands within the black community.

The major efforts to achieve self-determination have been made in the ghetto schools and on college campuses. From April, 1967, through November, 1968, there raged a bitter controversy between the local board of a demonstration district set up in the Ocean Hill-Brownsville section of Brooklyn and the predominantly Jewish United Federation of Teachers. The arguments for and against community control of schools and the Brooklyn controversy, itself, will be discussed in Chapter Seven. On campuses throughout the country from Cornell to California black students have been demanding their own departments of Afro-American studies and authority over curriculum and admissions policy insofar as blacks are affected. This issue will also be explored in Chapter Seven.

In Philadelphia, Rev. Leon Sullivan has accepted some aspects of self-determination and rejected others in his Opportunities Industrialization Center. Since 1964, the OIC, aided by government subsidy, has trained and placed in jobs 20,000 blacks, and, with funds from the black community, has set up what is perhaps the largest shopping center owned by blacks in the world. Now located in seventy cities, the OIC puts great emphasis on pride and self-respect and encourages black ownership of businesses in the ghetto (sometimes known as "black capitalism"). However, Rev. Sullivan favors desegregation and is interested not in changing the American economy but in enabling the black man to take his rightful place as entrepreneur and skilled worker.[24]

Out of the movement towards black self-determination there has emerged what Earl Raab has called "black expressivism," a tendency to express frustration through inflammatory rhetoric rather than to develop programs that would eliminate the causes of the frustration.[25] This anger has at times been expressed against Jews, and, by 1969, the issue of black anti-Semitism (how serious is it? how should Jews respond?) was being debated from the smooth pages of *Time* to the sophisticated columns of *Commentary*. This highly sensitive subject will be explored in some detail in Chapter Eight.

While the broader implications of the strategies of self-determination will be discussed in the last three chapters, the question of separatism versus coalition might now be explored. The younger black leaders have been charged with a go-it-alone psychology that can lead only to futility: after all, the black community is a minority in America. A. Philip Randolph has urged "coalition power": In order for poverty to be eliminated there must be a coalition of blacks together with progressive elements in the white community, e.g., the labor movement, the academic profession and religious groups. Together they would work for such massive anti-poverty programs as those proposed by the Freedom Budget (see Chapter Five). Max Lerner has written:

> There has been a distortion in this issue of power. I happen to believe that the problem of the Negro in America will not be resolved until the Negro has become part of the larger power structure in America. He must get rid of his sense of powerlessness but the way to do that is through integration and coalition politics. Separatism and exclusiveness lead to hatred and to polarization.[26]

Stokely Carmichael and Charles Hamilton have replied to such appeals by pointing to the "myths" of coalition: (1) that interests of black people are identical with the interests of other groups; (2) that the secure can make an effective coalition with the insecure (they cannot; their interests are different); (3) that coalitions can be sustained on a moral or sentimental basis. On the contrary, coalitions must be based on mutual interests, and the only whites whose vital interests are shared by blacks are the very poor. Elsewhere the authors have written: "Black Power . . . has no connotation of 'go-it-alone.' Black Power simply says: enter coalitions only after you are able to stand on your own." [27]

Discussion: Do you believe a materially secure person motivated by a genuine desire to relieve human suffering can join with the black or white poor to strive for public policies and programs that would eliminate poverty? What kinds of sacrifices would such a coalition require the secure person to make? In what ways are the interests of middle-class Americans in general and Jews in particular similar to and different from the interests of the poor blacks? Are the interests of middle-class blacks the same as those of poor blacks? How would a self-determinist persuade poor blacks who rose in the economic scale to continue working with their less fortunate brothers? What kinds of coalitions do you think are workable?

In the hope that the history of Jewish emancipation might shed some light on the issues dividing the black community, one might consider the strategies and goals of the Jewish community.

1.) When the Jews sought their rights did they go-it-alone or did they form coalitions? In Russia some Jews tried the coalition strategy as they joined the Russian Socialist movement! However, when non-Jewish workers turned against them in the pogroms of 1903-4, an increasing number of Jews separated from the mainstream of Russian socialism and turned to Labor Zionism with its goal of a Jewish state. However, even this separatist goal proved to be dependent first on the British foreign office and later on the United Nations. In western Europe and the United States, the Jewish people formed their own "defense organizations," dedicated to securing and safeguarding human rights for Jews. However, these groups worked closely with the liberal elements of the particular society which also had a great stake in the values of democracy.

Discussion: Assuming that the American Negro has no real possibility of establishing his own state, what does Jewish experience suggest about the policy of "going-it-alone"? If non-Jews have not participated in Jewish community relations agencies, why should whites expect to be part of groups primarily concerned with rights for Negroes? Is it possible that the "Black Revolution" might best be served by the simultaneous pursuit of both separatist and integrationist strategies?

2.) Has the Jewish goal been integration into the larger society or the development of a distinctively Jewish cultural life? Obviously both. Many Jewish people have found certain values in maintaining communal institutions and living in areas highly populated by Jews. These values range from having a feeling of belonging in an impersonal urban area to developing religious and cultural institutions that can express and perpetuate the ideals of the group. Louis Lomax, who has argued against such voluntary segregation, did recognize one of its by-products when he predicted that the first Negro congressman to be elected from a predominantly white constituency would probably come from a largely Jewish suburb. [28] However, while retaining their cultural identity, the Jews have achieved complete economic and political and a degree of social integration into the larger society. So, as for the goal of integration or separation, perhaps it is not a question of either-or.

Discussion: Can the American Negro find value in preserving his community and his cultural heritage? If so, will it be possible for him to integrate without assimilating into the American mainstream? For further thoughts on this and related questions, see Chapter Six.

"How Do You Answer a Revolution?"

The "Black Revolution" has moved from its first phase, a civil rights movement that secured equality before the law, into a struggle against the social and economic conditions that prevent the black man from achieving equality in fact. Because of the frustration that has come from the failure of the second phase of the revolt to make progress sufficient to be appreciated by the man in the slum, some groups within the black community have given up on the system. They have said, in effect: "If you will not let us in your world, then we will gain control of our own community and determine our own black destiny."

The challenge is clear: What does the white community really believe about equality? Who or what is, in fact, responsible for the high proportion of poverty among blacks? What programs would eliminate the miserable conditions that leave provoked blacks to turn inward and cry out in anger? These should be the prime concerns of the white American. Once these questions are honestly explored, it is then time to look more closely at the movement towards self-determination that is often viewed as a threat by whites in general and Jews in particular.

But first, in order to set our own house in order, let us turn to the ideal of equality, an ideal mouthed so frequently that it has become for many a platitude. Gunner Myrdal, the Swedish sociologist, has pointed out to Americans that they are caught on the horns of "the American dilemma." [29] On the one hand, Americans are, as a matter of conscience, committed to a creed that emphasizes the doctrine of equal rights. The Declaration of Independence is generally interpreted to mean that all Americans should be given equal opportunity to make the most of their talents and abilities. However, when citizens who do not, in fact, have such opportunity demand this right, other citizens may respond: No, one cannot push equality that far!*

An important part of the problem is that Americans differ widely in their interpretations of "equality" and "human rights." In the following chapter such terms will be examined in the context of the American creed, and this creed will then be viewed in the light of Jewish tradition.

---

* See Opinionaire Items 1 and 2. Many Americans hold attitudes which contradict this egalitarian ideal. For example, those who checked both Items 1 and 14 "Agree " would be saying that the right to the pursuit of happiness should not extend to the right of buying a home without being penalized by one's race. Those who checked both Items 2 and 16 "Agree " would deny that equality should extend to members of a group a significant portion of whom are irresponsible.

LEST WE FORGET

As the Jewish people have so often said of their own martyrs who died for the ideals of their faith, so let it be said of those Americans of whatever race or creed whose lives were lost in the struggle for freedom, "May their memory be for a blessing."

EMMET TILL, 14, Negro, murdered August 28, 1955.

MACK CHARLES PARKER, 23, Negro, lynched April 25, 1959.

WILLIAM L. MOORE, 35, white Baltimore postman, shot near Attalla, Ala., April 23, 1963.

MEDGAR W. EVERS, 37, NAACP field secretary, ambushed in Jackson, Miss., June 12, 1963.

DENISE McNAIR, 11, CYNTHIA WESLEY, CAROL ROBERTSON and ADDIE MAE COLLINS, 14, Negro schoolgirls, killed in church bombing, Birmingham, Ala., September 15, 1963.

JOHNNY ROBINSON, 16, Negro, killed by a policeman's shotgun after church bombing, Birmingham, Ala., September 15, 1963.

MICHAEL SCHWERNER, 24, and ANDREW GOODMAN, 20, both Northerners and white, and their Negro comrade, JAMES CHANEY, 21, of Meridian, Miss., disappeared on a June night in 1964. Their bodies were dug out of a redclay dam five miles from Philadelphia, Miss.

LEMUEL A. PENN, 49, Negro school official returning to Washington, D.C., from Army Reserve training, killed by a shotgun blast on a north Georgia highway, July 11, 1964.

JIMMIE LEE JACKSON, 26, Negro, according to witnesses, was shot by a state trooper while protecting his mother from a beating, Marion, Ala., February 18, 1965. Died, February 26.

REV. JAMES J. REEB, 38, white Boston Unitarian minister, clubbed, Selma, Ala., March 9, 1965. Died, March 11.

VIOLA GREGG LIUZZO, 39, white Detroit housewife, killed on U.S. Highway 80 near Selma, Ala., March 25, 1965, following Montgomery march.

VERNON DAHMER, 58, Negro, killed in firebombing of his home, Hattiesburg, Miss., January 10, 1966 following leadership of a voter registration drive.

THE REV. DR. MARTIN LUTHER KING, 39, Negro, murdered in Memphis, Tenn., April 4, 1968, director of the Southern Christian Leadership Conference, and the revered leader of the Civil Rights movement.

"I'VE SEEN THE PROMISED LAND"

These are the words of Rev. Martin Luther King, spoken in Memphis, Tenn., April 3, 1968...the day before he was murdered....

". . .and then I got to Memphis. And some began to talk about the threats that were out. Or what would happen to me from some of our sick white brothers.

Well, I don't know what will happen now. We've got some difficult days ahead. But it really doesn't matter with me now. Because I've been to the mountain top. I won't mind.

Like anybody, I would like to live a long life. Longevity has its place. But I'm not concerned about that now. I just want to do God's will.

And He's allowed me to go up to the mountain. And I've looked over, and I've seen the promised land.

I may not get there with you, but I want you to know tonight that we as a people will get to the promised land.

So I'm happy tonight. I'm not worried about anything. I'm not fearing any man. Mine eyes have seen the glory of the coming of the Lord."

These names were compiled largely by Charles Morgan, Jr., for *Look* Magazine, June 29, 1965. There were undoubtedly others who lost their lives because of racism.

Chapter Three

WHAT DO YOU REALLY BELIEVE ABOUT EQUALITY?

"Do you believe in the Declaration of Independence?"

"Of course, doesn't everybody?"

The fact is that most Americans mechanically quote the ringing words of the declaration without having any clear idea of what they mean. "All men are created equal"—but are there not differences in inherited capacities? "They are endowed by their Creator with certain unalienable rights"— How do we know God endowed us, and what *are* "unalienable rights"? "Among these are life, liberty, and the pursuit of happiness"—Does this mean there are others? What happens when my unalienable rights conflict with yours? Whatever one may say of the declaration, its truths are far from self-evident.

In this chapter we shall attempt to understand the meaning of equality and human rights in the light of the American creed and our Jewish tradition. In what sense are all men equal? What is meant by human rights, civil rights, economic rights? How do Americans differ over the meanings of "equal opportunity" and "property rights"?

We shall then consult Judaism, its theology, ethics, history, and law, as we attempt to answer two important questions posed by the doctrine of equal rights: Why should one care about the rights of anyone other than himself? How should one go about resolving conflicts between rights?

The Meaning of Equality

What does a person mean when he says, "I'm just as good as the next fellow"? He usually does not mean, "I'm just as smart or as strong or as moral." Yet, he feels that in some basic intangible sense, he *is* his neighbor's equal. But in what sense?

"I'm just as good as the next fellow" is another way of saying: "I am just as entitled as he is to certain basic rights." For example, if he has the right to free speech (so long as his words do not pose a clear and present danger to society), then I should have the very same right. To say "I'm just as good as the next fellow" means also that "he is just as good as I am." That is, whatever I claim as my basic right, he may also claim as *his* basic right.

Therefore, the statement, "all men are created equal," does not mean that men are born with the same talents or capacities. It means that all men are born with the same claim to certain fundamental rights.[1] To define human equality in this manner, however, is to raise a host of questions.

On Defining Our Rights

Among philosophers and political scientists there is considerable disagreement as to how the rights of man should be defined and classified. "Human rights" have been defined by philosopher-educator Harry S. Broudy as "claims that flow from and are certified by our membership in the human race."[2] These are the rights without which we would not be human. Since we are human, according to Broudy, by virtue of our rational powers (thinking, speaking, imagining, striving, etc.), then when we are deprived of the ability to express these powers, we are being deprived of our very humanity. Such rights are, therefore, inseparable (or unalienable) from our *nature*. Therefore, they are natural or human rights.

The United Nations Declaration of Human Rights contains two categories: (1) political or civil; and (2) social and economic. The "political or civil" rights are intended primarily to protect the individual from state action that would deny his basic human aspirations. These would include the rights to marry, to equality before the law, and to free

[39]

speech and assembly. Economic and social rights pertain to earning a livelihood and enjoying those benefits society should provide for all its members. The U.N. Declaration includes in this category: to form trade unions, to receive equal pay for equal work, and even to go on periodic holidays with pay.

Such social and economic rights may easily become the subject of endless debate. Would the denial of these rights really mean the denial of one's humanity? A British political scientist, Maurice Cranston, has criticized the U.N. Declaration for lumping together fundamental human rights with less than fundamental social goals (e.g., holidays with pay).[3]

Since it is not always clear that specific social and economic rights are absolutely essential to one's humanity, some philosophers are content to say: Let each society determine which rights its citizens may claim. This determination will be based on the felt needs of the people and the capacity of the society to meet those needs. In highly industrial cultures, people may claim the right to form a union or to have medicare for the elderly. Such claims would have no meaning in a nonindustrial culture. Once the determination of rights is made by popular consensus, *then all citizens should have an equal claim to those rights.*[4] For example, if Americans generally claim the right to adequate public school facilities for their children through high school, then this claim cannot be denied to any particular racial, religious or economic group. In other words, what you claim as a right for yourself, you should also recognize as a right for your neighbor!

To sum up: Human rights are generally defined as those claims essential to one's humanity. However, now that some societies are so productive that they can provide their citizens with benefits that go beyond that which is minimally required for one to be human, the emphasis is often shifted from the classical concept of human rights to the notion of equality, itself: Let the society determine its own rights, and let all its members receive *equal* treatment.

Equal Opportunity and Property Rights

The most highly prized right in America today is probably the right to equal opportunity. In the words of Sidney Hook:

> The principle of equality is not a description of fact about men's physical or intellectual natures. . . . It is equality of opportunity for all individuals to develop whatever personal and socially desirable talents they possess and to make whatever unique contributions their capacities permit.5

This does not mean that everyone should be treated in identical ways regardless of his capacities. A musical genius is entitled to greater opportunities to develop his talent than the person who is tone deaf. What is equal is the *concern* shown to each human being, that he might realize his potential to the fullest.

Americans are, however, divided as to how they interpret the ideal of "equal opportunity." For some, the phrase means that all individuals should have the same legal right to compete freely in the game of life. This is the view of the "classical or *laissez faire*" liberal. The "modern or welfare" liberal would interpret equal opportunity to mean *real,* rather than simply legal, equality. For example, the slum child, while equal under the law, does not have, *in fact,* the same opportunity for self-fulfillment as the child growing up in the suburbs.

At the center of much civil rights controversy is the concept of "property rights." According to what Russel Kirk calls "the conservative mind," the right to one's possessions is the most fundamental of all human rights. John Adams held that equality means "every being has *a right to his own,* as moral, as sacred as any other has."6 Adams' views were similar to those of the Englishman, Edmund Burke, who maintained that the foremost natural right was the right to justice and order, and that true justice means "to each his own."7

The conservative tradition, traceable to Adams and Burke, which emphasizes property rights frequently comes into conflict with the modern liberal position that stresses real equality of opportunity for a man to fulfill his potential. Sometimes this is labeled as a clash between property rights and human rights. However, as has been noted, property rights are considered by many conservatives to be the most basic of human rights. At any rate, the right of one person to do as he pleases with his property can easily come into conflict with someone else's right to satisfy what he considers a basic human need. For example, should an individual be able to sell his home to anyone he wishes? Or, is it more important that another individual be able to live where he can afford without being excluded because of his race?

Judaism and Equal Rights

Thus far in this chapter we have discussed the meaning of "equality," "human rights," and other concepts that are central to the understanding of the "Black Revolution." However, having defined our terms, we are immediately faced with two very serious questions: (1) Do we really believe in equal rights, and, if so, why? (2) What should we do when there are conflicts between one's own rights and the rights of his neighbor? In the remainder of this chapter we shall approach these questions in the light of Jewish belief and experience.

Why Believe in Equality?

Equality has been defined as the concept that all men are born with the same claim to certain fundamental rights. This is what is meant by the common sentiment, "I'm just as good as the next fellow." One might call this the "equality-feeling." However, not everyone has such a feeling. There are many "detached Americans" who see no reason at all why the rights they demand for themselves should also be the rights of their neighbors. "If giving the slum dweller's child true equality of opportunity means raising my taxes, why should I bother?" The challenge can be stated in more general terms: "I have enough problems of my own. Why should I worry about the world?"

1. The Biblical Foundation of the Equal Rights Doctrine

The Declaration of Independence states that "all men are created equal, and are endowed by their Creator with certain unalienable rights." Thus, one of the roots of the equal rights doctrine of the American creed may be traced back to the biblical concept of the creation of man. But how so?

According to the Torah, man was created in the image of God, that is, with a soul that is an expression of the Divine in man. That God has planted in the heart of man a spark of His spirit was, according to the rabbis, a sign that *God loves man:* "Beloved is man of God, for he was created in the image of God."[8] It would then follow that if God cares for all His children, we, too, should do our best to love them. A rabbi and philosopher, Emil Fackenheim, has stated this idea in terms of personal experience:

> . . . in discovering in the God-man encounter that *we* matter before God, we at the same time discover that *every man matters.* In being responsible to God, we are also responsible to each other.[9]

For Rabbi Robert Gordis, the belief that all life is "equally the creation of God" is sufficient reason for regarding other lives as having an equal right to fulfillment.[10]

The Bible, itself, provides many examples of concern for the rights of others. The classic expression of human equality is, of course, the commandment in Leviticus— 19:18: "Thou shalt love thy neighbor as thyself." In the twenty-fourth chapter, equality under the law is clearly implied.

> Ye shall have one manner of law, as well for the stranger as for the home-born; for I am the Lord your God.[11]

For example, the stranger, if he be poor, is just as entitled as is the home-born to the charitable support of the community.[12] It must be admitted that the Mosaic law did not always reflect the principle of human equality that was so deeply rooted in biblical theology and ethics. These inconsistencies, real or apparent, between individual Jewish laws and the ideals of Jewish morality will be explored later in this chapter.

The principle of human equality was preserved through the covenant, the contract which the Israelites believed they had made with God and which bound them throughout all their generations to do His will. In each generation, we have fallen short in our lives and our laws, but the goal is still there: To love one's neighbor as oneself and to build a just society based on this equalitarian principle.

Discussion: Do you believe that each of us "matters before God"? Assuming that all life is "equally the creation of God," does it, therefore, follow that other lives have the same right to fulfillment as your own? Do you believe that Israel has a covenant with God to do His will throughout all their generations? How do the beliefs and experiences of the biblical Jews affect you?

2. Some Naturalistic Bases for Equal Rights

Not all Jews today can accept the belief in a God who is lovingly aware of each of His children and who chose Israel to be His people. Those who cannot share this faith have often turned to "naturalistic" reasons for believing in equal rights, that is, reasons that depend not on the existence of a supernatural deity, but on conclusions drawn from experience in the natural world.

While America's founding fathers invoked God as the author of human rights, they were also very strongly influenced by the seventeenth-century Englishman, John Locke, who based his philosophy on experience within the realm of nature. Locke had compared the mind to a *tabula rasa,* a completely blank tablet, and had maintained that whatever was learned came from experience. A number of eighteenth-century thinkers concluded from this that since all that men are comes from experience, all inequalities must be due to different experiences; therefore, men at birth must be exactly equal.[13]

In the nineteenth century, Jeremy Bentham came to believe that a just society could be built on the principle of utility: A community should be so ordered as to make for the greatest happiness for the greatest number. The philosopher of Reconstructionist Judaism, Mordecai Kaplan, who considers happiness to be self-fulfillment, has offered what could be considered a twentieth century version of the utilitarian standard. Rabbi Kaplan has defined "social salvation" as "the ultimate achievement of a social order in which all men shall collaborate in the pursuit of common ends *in a manner which shall afford to each the maximum opportunity for creative self-expression.*"[14]

The problem with the utilitarian approach arises when one asks the question: Why should I want to build a society in which *everyone* will have the maximum opportunity for self-expression? Why should I not be satisfied with an imperfect world in which I, at least, may find fulfillment? One response may be that the only way one can be sure of having such opportunity for oneself is to live in a society where *everyone* has such opportunity. Also, when one considers the violence that has resulted from the denial of certain rights, one might maintain that so long as there is such denial, no one will be able to live a life free of anxiety and fear.

Rabbi Kaplan would not rest with such arguments but would state that one's sense of responsibility for his fellowman is rooted in the principle of interdependence in the cosmos itself, and that the attitude of love is part of certain cooperative and organic tendencies in nature. Not only is a sense of moral responsibility and love useful (indeed, essential) for achieving human happiness, but these values also have their foundation in the universe, itself. To believe that by following these ideals, which are rooted both in men's inner nature and in the cosmos, one may discover the "life abundant" is to believe in God.

Discussion: Is it true that the individual can be assured of a happy creative life only if all other members of the community have their rights? How would you answer the detached American who might respond to such arguments by saying: "I'm quite comfortable in my suburban home. Why should I be bothered by an occasional riot in the slums?" How are all Americans, wherever they may live, affected by a denial of human rights?

3. To be Fully Human Is to Believe in Equal Rights

Should none of the foregoing arguments be convincing, one might finally respond with some exasperation: "If you deny your fellowman the same rights you claim for yourself, then you are not really human!" But what is meant by being "really human"? A. H. Maslow considers the fully human person to be one who is psychologically healthy, whose basic needs of safety, love, and self-esteem have been met and who is able to be spontaneously creative. Such "self-actualized" persons will, *in fact,* care about the rights of others. Maslow claims that the psychologically healthy people he has studied do have "a deep feeling of identification, sympathy, and affection (and) a genuine desire to help the human race. It is as if they were all members of a single family."[15] Conversely, if you lack such feelings, you are not fully human.

Although approaching the problem of detachment from a different perspective, the great Jewish philosopher, Martin Buber, reflected this psychological point of view when he wrote:

It is an idle undertaking to call out to a mankind that has grown blind to eternity: "Look! the eternal values!" One has to begin by pointing to the relation of the individual to his own self . . . *it is first necessary to be a person again.*[16]

One who is not a real person will be incapable of caring. However, the man whose human potential has fully developed

[46]

will be concerned with the rights of his fellowman. As Rabbi Kaplan has maintained, there are certain spiritual processes in man which include moral responsibility, love, honesty, and creativity and which are rooted in nature-as-a-whole.17 The man in whom these processes have not fully developed has not become fully human. To state this in more traditional terms: God has given man a heart for loving. The man who cannot love is missing an essential dimension of human life and is not fulfilling his God-given nature. Perhaps that is why the commandment, "Love thy neighbor as thyself," is followed by the simple statement: "I am the Lord."

4. Jewish History and Equal Rights

As Jews, our history provides us with a reason for developing a special sensitivity to the needs of our neighbors. The Torah reads:

> And a stranger shalt thou not oppress, for ye know the heart of the stranger, seeing ye were strangers in the land of Egypt.18

If, as a Jew, your heart is moved by the sufferings of the Jewish people, then you might also be expected to feel compassion for any other group of "strangers" who are oppressed.

The Jew was, of course, a stranger in more lands than Egypt. He lived in exile by the Euphrates and by the Nile, but it was in medieval Europe that he became the scapegoat of the Western world. Excluded from guilds (the unions of those days), he was forced into petty money lending and a few marginal crafts. So, today, Negroes have been excluded from so many unions that while the exceptionally talented may become a doctor, lawyer or diplomat, the average but capable often cannot become a mechanic, a stone-mason or an electrician.

Like the Negro, we Jews have known the false accusation, followed by murder. For us, it was the charge of killing Christian children, followed by the pogrom. For the Negro, it was often the charge of rape followed by the lynch mob.

[47]

It is true that no madman has tried to exterminate the Negro race, but the parallels between the Nazi terror and the American slave trade are more startling than we may realize. When Negroes were brought from the heart of Africa to the American South, one-third died enroute to the African coast and one-third died in the suffocating prisons on board ship. Once here, families were purposely broken up; husbands, wives, and children forced to go their separate ways. Must we be reminded of the death toll in the suffocating boxcars bound for Auschwitz or of the tearing of children from their mothers' arms. Professor Stanley Elkins of the University of Chicago has pointed out that the inmates of the concentration camps became submissive, docile, infantile, and even began aping and flattering their masters. This, Professor Elkins observed, was precisely how the Negro behaved when his ego collapsed under the oppressive weight of the Southern slave system.[19] Finally, during the holocaust, the Jewish people knew (as the Negro knows today) the cold indifference of the silent majority. As Jews, we *have* known the heart of the stranger. Therefore, we *should* be sensitive to the needs of the American Negro. *But are we?*[20]

Discussion: Do all people react to suffering in the same way? Obviously not. Some may develop compassion for the oppressed of the world while others may conclude: Nobody helped us, so why should we help *them?* According to Gordon Allport, "being a victim oneself disposes one either to develop aggression toward *or* sympathy with other out-groups."[21]

Under what circumstances might a person become embittered by suffering? Under what circumstances might a person become more tolerant as a result of experiencing discrimination? How has Judaism encouraged the Jewish people to transform suffering into compassion for others who suffer?

Equal Rights in Jewish Law

Thus far we have seen that the theology, the ethics, and the history of Judaism all tend to support the doctrine of equal

[48]

rights. Whether one believes with the traditionalist that God is the loving Creator of all men or with the naturalist that God is the process that makes for the creative self-expression of all men, one is led to advocate equal rights. All theologies within Judaism consider "Love thy neighbor as thyself," to be a basic moral principle that clearly implies equality. The historic experiences of the Jewish people with oppression have made it possible for many Jews to become particularly sensitive to the needs of all who are denied their rights. But what of Jewish law?

The purpose of the law was to bring the ideals of Torah into the lives and institutions of the people; and yet, the rabbis were only human. To what extent did they succeed in translating the equal rights doctrine into reality? Let us begin by admitting that Jewish law was not always consistent with the ideal.

The most dramatic example of such inconsistency was perhaps slavery. Both biblical and rabbinic law permitted Jews to own slaves in all ages wherever slavery was the general practice. It has been suggested that during certain historical periods because of primitive productive techniques, free labor alone could not keep the economy going; therefore, slavery was a necessity. Whether slavery was essential for the community's existence or whether it was the most profitable means of social organization for the ruling classes may be debated. What *is* clear is that Jewish law required unusually considerate treatment for slaves. For example, in contrast to the fugitive slave law passed by Congress in 1854, Deuteronomy insists that he who "is escaped from his master unto thee shall dwell with thee . . . thou shalt not oppress him."22 Living in a society where slavery was an established institution, the Jews could hardly be expected to eliminate it. The rabbis did attempt, within the limits of their historic situation, to make sure that the slave was regarded with the dignity and respect befitting a child of God.

Still there was one law regarding slaves that opens up the whole question of discrimination against non-Jews:

Hebrew slaves were freed every seven years (a worthy humanitarian measure), while non-Hebrew slaves remained in bondage![23] To understand the formidable question of the treatment of the Gentile in Jewish law, one should realize that this law was naturally influenced by the social conditions under which the Jews lived, conditions that at times made it difficult if not impossible to translate the ideal of equal rights into the statutes of the community.

During the talmudic period the Jews lived either in Palestine or in self-governing communities within the Parthian Empire. The outside world appeared as a threat for two reasons: There was the danger of attack or persecution by the dominant power and the fear that contact with non-Jews might encourage neglect of traditional practice. As might have been expected, Jewish law did at times reflect this suspicion of the gentile world. For example, according to Rabbi Ishmael, a Jew was legally bound to restore a lost article he had found *only* if its owner were Jewish, but not if the article had belonged to a Gentile. While to modern ears, this ruling sounds unfair, to the talmudic Jew, whose property was often appropriated by the non-Jew, such a law appeared as a just form of retaliation.[24] Other kinds of talmudic "discrimination" against the non-Jew included: He could not serve as an agent for a Jew in a legal transaction; he could not buy cattle from a Jew; he *could* be charged an exorbitant price (termed: *ona'ah* or over-reaching), while a Jew could not be so charged.[25]

On the other hand, the Talmud contains many statutes that do safeguard the rights of non-Jews. In *Gittin* we read:

> We support the poor of the heathen along with the poor of Israel and visit the sick of the heathen along with the sick of Israel and bury the dead of the heathen along with the dead of Israel for the sake of peace.[26]

In the case of the *ger toshav,* the resident alien, it is our duty to see that he earns a livelihood. We are forbidden to withhold his salary or to steal from him, and we permit him to acquire land in Israel.[27]

When Jews began to settle throughout Europe, they were, contrary to popular impression, rather well treated until the end of the eleventh century. Living in extremely small communities (often less than ten and rarely more than one hundred souls), they naturally had many daily contacts with non-Jews, especially of a business nature. Consequently, certain "discriminatory" laws were interpreted in a more liberal manner or abolished altogether. Rabbi Ishmael's view that a Gentile's property is not under the protection of Jewish law (see above) was discarded in favor of Rabbi Akiba's interpretation that the Gentile is entitled to equal protection under the law for all his possessions. The early mishnaic law forbidding Jews to sell cattle to non-Jews was considered no longer binding, since such a ruling would, under new conditions, entail an economic loss for the Jew.[28]

Then came the first and second Crusades (1096 and 1146) when Christian armies pillaged Jewish communities and slaughtered their inhabitants on the way to the Holy Land. As one might expect, in some communities, there was considerably less enthusiasm for the protection of gentile rights. For example, in the *Sefer Chasidim,* a book of rules written by a Rav Judah for the pietists of the twelfth century, a Jew, who was commanded to desecrate the Sabbath to save the life of a fellow-Jew, was prohibited from committing even a minor violation of the Sabbath to save the life of a Gentile![29] Contrast this attitude with that of the twelfth-century philosopher Moses Maimonides, who, although forced to flee from the Almohadean regime in Spain, was heir to the intellectual world of a happier age, a world that led him to conclude that all men may, after diligent study, receive divine ideas from God. So, Maimonides declared in his *Mishnah Torah:*

> Jew and non-Jew are to be treated alike. If the vendor knows that his merchandise is defective, he must so inform the purchaser (whatever his religion).[30]

Influenced by the Maimonidean philosophic tradition, Rabbi Menahem Meiri of Provence ruled in the fourteenth century that a Jew *should* desecrate the Sabbath to save the life of a non-Jew, any law to the contrary having been intended only for ancient times when non-Jews were heathens and had no sense of duty to society. (Meiri's decision was quoted not long ago by Chief Rabbi Unterman of Israel when he issued a responsum vigorously denying a charge raised by a Dr. Shahak that Jewish law prohibits transgressing the Sabbath to save a Gentile's life.)[31]

Rabbi Moses Rivkes, lured from Wilna in the seventeenth century by the first hints of enlightenment in the West, responded to the more tolerant atmosphere by writing that because Christians also worshipped God, we should not only save them from danger but should pray for their welfare and the success of their governments. In the cosmopolitan atmosphere of the eighteenth century, R. Ezekiel Landau ruled in a responsum:

> I emphatically declare that in all laws contained in the Jewish writings concerning theft, fraud, etc., no distinction is made between Jew and Gentile; that the titles *goy, akum,* (idolater) etc., in no wise apply to the people among whom we live.

The discriminatory laws of the Talmud had no place in the modern world.[32]

In this brief survey of equal rights doctrine in Jewish law, we have drawn a distinction between the ideal of human equality, implied by the theology and ethics of Judaism, and the rabbinic laws which, for understandable reasons, did not always reflect that ideal. We might conclude that the law most clearly reflected the equality principle during periods when Jews were well integrated into the life of the larger society and when there was relatively little anti-Jewish discrimination or persecution.

Discussion: America also has a creed based on the ideal of equality. Looking back over American history, can you recall any federal or state laws that contradicted this creed?

Having suggested the various foundations that Judaism provides for the doctrine of equal rights, we turn to the question:
How should one resolve a conflict in which both parties consider their irreconcilable claims to be human rights? Because
of its frequent involvement in civil rights controversy, we
shall take as our example the clash between the right to do
whatever one wishes with his property and any human right
considered essential to someone else's well-being.

Jewish law assumes the existence of private property
and protects the owner's right to legitimate possession, in the
spirit of *Mishnah Avot:* "Let the property of thy neighbor
be as dear to thee as thine own."[33] However, in both Bible
and Talmud there are numerous instances in which the right
to do as one pleases with his property is clearly limited by
other human rights. According to the Torah, if one builds
a house, he is required to erect a parapet for the roof, lest
someone fall and be injured or killed. The rabbis not only
specified the size and strength of the parapet but also prohibited a person from having pits, trenches, ditches or caves
on his own property, lest these prove hazardous.[34] According
to one medieval authority, it was even illegal to have on
one's property a defective ladder or a vicious dog![35] Examples of such limitations on property rights could be multi-
plied, from the law that if one had a well on his grounds, he
had to make the water available to the inhabitants of the
nearby community to the previously stated statute that the
farmer was required to set aside a corner of his field for the
poor.[36] Evidently the rabbis valued human life, health, and
safety above the right to do as one pleases with his possessions.

Property rights did not always give way to the claim
of other human rights. Was not the institution of slavery a
case in which the right to one's "property" was elevated
above the right of a human being to be free? As has been
noted, some might argue that the existence of the economy
depended on there being slaves; therefore, the suppression of
some human freedom was regrettably essential. Similarly,

today certain restrictions against private property are opposed on the grounds that they would lead to the end of our
economic system, and so unfortunately lesser human rights
must be sacrificed. To make a judgment in each case, one has
to examine just what the consequences of limiting the
property rights in question would really be.

To view the conflict between property rights and other
human rights in the light of Jewish ethics, we might attempt
to apply the commandment, "Love thy neighbor as thyself"
to particular situations. Assuming the commandment means
that the well-being of one's neighbor should be considered
as important as one's own, the question then becomes: So
long as one of you must give up a cherished claim, who, on
giving up his claim, would suffer less? Or, if you would
consider every man to be your neighbor: How would people
in general be affected if your right (then: if your neighbor's
right) were limited? In which case would there be "the
maximum opportunity for creative self-expression"?

Discussion: How might the following conflict between property rights
and other human rights be resolved in a manner consistent with Jewish
ethical principles:

a) Gun control legislation.

b) Private will versus public policy: There have been a number of
cases in which private individuals many decades ago bequeathed large
grants of money to educational institutions with the stipulation that
the schools would be open to whites only. In view of changes in public
policy, these wills have been challenged in the courts, so that the
schools might be opened to all races (e.g., the Girard College case in
Philadelphia).

c) The right to serve whomever you please in one's place of
business versus the right to be served regardless of one's race.

"The Jewish Dilemma"

Thus far we have indicated that Judaism does provide a
theological, moral, and historical foundation for the doctrine
of equal rights, and that our faith also offers not answers

but guides that can help us resolve the conflicts between rights. However, despite the affirmation of the ideal of human equality we may persist in acting in ways contrary to that ideal—a kind of Jewish version of Myrdal's "American Dilemma." To give an example from real life:

In the early 1960's several members of CORE were attempting to desegregate an amusement park by means of nonviolent demonstrations. The owner of the park was a Jew whose family had come from the same part of the Ukraine as had the family of one of the CORE workers, who was also Jewish. The two struck up a conversation in Yiddish, and the park owner proceeded to tell his coreligionist from CORE that *he* knew what persecution was; his relatives had been imprisoned in concentration camps; some were killed by the Nazis. And he added in the same breath, "Now will you please tell your friends to get out of here?"37

Most people do have feelings of compassion. They want to help their fellowman in need. They do, in a part of their hearts, cherish the ideal of human equality. Yet, for various reasons they act in ways that contradict the ideal. In the next chapter, we shall examine some of the reasons most frequently offered for resisting the demand of the "Black Revolution" for real equality.

Chapter Four

THE QUESTION OF RESPONSIBILITY

"I am sick and tired of hearing about the plight of the poor Negro. So he had a rough deal. So plenty of people have had rough deals. If he'd stay in school long enough to get educated he'd get along. Sure, I know there's discrimination, but if more Negroes would just learn to be responsible law-abiding citizens, there wouldn't be so much prejudice.

"Why don't they start helping themselves? My grandfather came from the old country with a pack on his back. That's all, just a pack and he couldn't even speak English. But his kids didn't become delinquents. Yes, we Jews were poor and they called us kikes, but we stayed in school. We didn't have any war against poverty to give us hand-outs, but we studied hard and we *deserved* our freedom! Let the Negro stop demanding and start earning his rights!"

If There's a Will, There's a Way

Such sentiments emphasize the Negro's responsibility for his own plight. That he faces many obstacles is granted, but these obstacles could be overcome by sufficient effort and willpower. Evidently the Negro slumdweller lacks the drive to improve himself, as others have done. In a phrase, "if there's a will, there's a way."*

---

*See Opinionaire Items 5, 7, 9, and 16. Agreement with these statements indicates acceptance of the view that the Negro is fundamentally responsible for his present lot.

[56]

If There's a Way, There's a Will

The social scientist explains the Negro's plight by pointing to the particular conditions he has been subjected to since arriving in this country. According to this sociological view, people are as they are primarily because of the sum total of experiences they have undergone. A close study of the experiences of the American Negro should, therefore, explain his low condition in the dark ghetto, including the apparent lack of will power and the delinquency. In fact, if conditions could be sufficiently altered, so that the slumdweller actually believed he had a realistic chance to share in the "affluent society," his will power would soon become manifest. That is to say, if there's a way, there's a will.

In this chapter we shall examine the claims of both hypotheses: (1) The Negro community is fundamentally responsible for its own plight; (2) The conditions experienced by the Negro community are fundamentally "responsible" for its tragic poverty. We shall then be in a better position to respond intelligently to the demand for real equality.

The Assumption Behind Negro Responsibility

If the first hypothesis is correct, that the Negro himself is primarily "to blame" for his plight, then the question arises: How can one explain his inability to improve his lot? To respond that he lacks the intelligence or will power is to raise the further question: Why does he lack these qualities? Now, if this lack cannot be explained by the conditions he has experienced (2nd hypothesis), there is only one other explanation: These deficiencies are racial characteristics of the Negro, who is, therefore, by birth inferior to the white man. Caucasians, not being deficient in will power and intelligence, have been able to overcome obstacles, while Negroes, because of innate racial qualities, have tended to remain a primitive people.

[57]

The biblical story of the creation of man provided the rabbis with a means of denying the validity of racism. Since, according to the ancient tradition, we are all descended from Adam, then, said our sages, no one has the right to boast of his superior ancestry. A *midrash* further states: "God formed Adam of dust from all over the world: Yellow clay and white sand, black loam, and red soil . . . ."[1] The implication is clear: All men, of whatever complexion, have a common origin. Since we are all equally related to Adam, our "Adamhood" (that is, our common humanity) is more fundamental than our racial differences. This insight has been verified by virtually all social scientists who have studied the relation between race and human nature.

Ashley Montagu, an anthropologist whose writings on race summarize the findings of the scholarly community, reminds us that IQ tests cannot possibly measure native intelligence. How one scores on such tests depends not only on inherited capacity but also on the opportunities one has had to learn, on how meaningful the items on the test are to the individual, and on how well one wants to do and can do in a test situation. What such tests do demonstrate is that "when the members of different groups are afforded similar opportunities for mental development, *the range of inherited capacities appears to be similar in all such groups.* Furthermore, the greater the learning opportunities of a group, the higher its members will score."[2]

For example, in tests given to American soldiers in World War I, the average score of the Negroes from six Northern states was higher than the average score of whites from fourteen Southern states. This suggests not that Northern Negroes are inherently superior to Southern whites but that conditions experienced by Negroes in the North gave them more opportunities for learning than did conditions experienced by Southern whites. In New Haven in 1946, a study was made comparing the intelligence of infants. So long as the social and economic background and the diet of the mother were the same, there was no significant difference between the scores of the Negro and white babies.[3]

The popular view that members of a particular group tend to have certain traits of temperament (e.g., laziness, sense of rhythm) because of their racial inheritance—this is considered by social scientists to be totally false. White children captured and raised by Indians were reported to have developed the "stolid" Indian temperament. Evidently, the Indian's "impassive nature" was due not to his genes but to his cultural environment.[4] Studies have also shown that crime is clearly a result not of inborn racial traits but of adverse social conditions. In Los Angeles, in 1956, Mexican-American boys from poor homes violated the law at about the same rate as did Negro boys from similar backgrounds.[5]

There is general agreement among scholars that there is absolutely no basis for believing in the inherent superiority of the white race. Two dissenters, Henry Garret and Audrey Shuey, have attempted to show that even when economic conditions are similar, Negroes make lower scores on intelligence tests than do whites.[6] However, as a chorus of social scientists was quick to point out, Garret and Shuey did not take into account that the Negro is disadvantaged not only because of his poverty but also because of discrimination, family instability and his recent arrival in the city. Martin Deutsch has shown that when Negro and white children were matched for social and economic class *only,* whites scored higher on mental tests, but when family stability and length of residence in the city were held constant in both groups, there were no significant differences between whites and Negroes.[7]

The latest argument for the view that the white race is by its biological nature more amply endowed with intelligence than the black race has been made by geneticist Arthur Jensen. Professor Jensen cited a study of a number of pairs of identical twins, each of whom was reared in a different environment, ranging from the richest to the poorest homes in England. Since identical twins have the same genetic endowment, this was considered a good opportunity to measure the relative influence of environment and inheritance on intelligence. It was found that the correlation between the IQ's of related twins reared separately was .75, while the correlation between the IQ's of nonrelated children reared together was .24.* This demonstrates, claimed Jensen, that heredity is of far greater importance than environment in determining IQ. He then jumped to the conclusion that IQ differences between population groups must be due largely to genetic (as opposed to environmental) differences between the groups.

Not so, replied psychologist Jerome Kagan: height, for example, is strongly influenced by heredity, but rural Indians were found to be smaller than urban Indians not because of genetic differences but because of the different nutritional environment in the cities. In other words, when there is severe environmental deprivation, characteristics such as height or intelligence (despite their high "heritability" factor) are dramatically affected. Such deprivation surely does exist in the life experience of the slum child. It is worth noting that in the British study cited by Jensen, none of the twins, while from different economic classes, were raised from birth experiencing the terrible conditions in the American black ghetto. Professor Jensen, while admitting the great effect of severe deprivation on IQ, refused to consider the slum child *that* deprived, a view that educational psychologist Lee Cronbach found difficult to understand: e.g., when small girls are locked in apartments to keep them away from the danger of the streets, or when children are raised without fathers by overburdened and undereducated working mothers, surely this *is* extreme deprivation.

Professor Jensen has also been criticized by his colleagues for not dealing adequately with the abundant experimental data that contradicts his thesis. For example, Professor I.I. Gottesman, a leading behavioral geneticist, noted that the differences between the IQ scores of thirty-eight identical twins reared in different environments was *larger* than the average IQ difference between black and

---

*Correlation is a measure of association. Perfect association scores one. Complete nonassociation scores zero.

white populations! It seems that IQ differences between black and white groups *can* be explained without considering the genetic factor to be significant. It has also been strongly suggested that the lower IQ scores of lower-class children are in considerable measure due to their culturally induced ignorance of what to do on tests. Dr. Francis Palmer, in one experiment, found that when examiners took sufficient time with the children to make sure they were relaxed and understood the procedures, there was no significant difference between the scores of lower-class and middle-class children! So, even the tests, themselves, may not reveal as much about intelligence as has often been assumed. In short, Professor Jensen, while joyfully quoted by a number of politically conservative columnists, has not been able to convince the overwhelming majority of his academic colleagues.*

A less scholarly argument for the view that the achievements of racial groups are largely genetically determined has been made by Carl Putnam, who has popularized the views of Garret and Shuey. Putnam has argued that the Negro race has not produced a literary work as fine as *Paradise Lost* or *David Copperfield*. His implication, that cultural achievement is a result of inherent racial traits, cannot be borne out by history. The English were culturally underdeveloped when the Egyptians and Babylonians were flourishing. England finally blossomed not because of some change in the biological endowment of British genes but because (among other reasons) the English came into contact with other peoples and this contact made possible economic growth and eventually a sophisticated level of literary creativity.

In Equatorial Africa, the torrid weather, the lack of waterways that make possible travel and communication, and the abundance of food that left few needs unsatisfied were all factors that inhibited the economic development which makes possible a literate culture.

---

*For a full discussion of this debate, see A. Jensen, "How Much Can We Boost IQ and Scholastic Achievement." *Harvard Educational Review*, Vol. 39:1, Winter, 1969, and articles by J. Kagan, J. F. Crow, L. Cronbach and others in *Harvard Educational Review*, Vol. 39:1, Spring, 1969.

The conclusion of virtually all reputable social scientists has been summarized by the UNESCO statement on race, drawn up by the world's foremost experts:

> As for personality and character, these may be considered raceless. In every human group, a rich variety of personality and character types will be found, and there is no reason for believing that any human group is richer than any other in these respects . . . .
>
> The scientific evidence indicates that the range of mental capacities in all ethnic groups is much the same . . . . Genetic differences are not of importance in determining the social and cultural differences between different groups of *homo sapiens.* [8]

Since there is no scientific basis on which one can establish the doctrine of inherent racial inferiority, advocates of this view have often attempted to find their justification in the Bible, which can, of course, be quoted on both sides of many questions. The so-called "curse of Ham," according to biblical tradition the ancestor of the Ethiopians and other dark-skinned people, has been invoked to "explain Negro inferiority." However, a close reading of the ninth chapter of *Genesis* will reveal that Ham, the son of Noah who saw his father naked and in a drunken stupor, was never cursed! It was Ham's son, Canaan, who received the curse and Canaan was the ancestor not of the Ethiopians but of the Canaanites. The Ethiopians were descended from one of Ham's other sons, Cush! Apparently the biblical author wanted to justify Israel's conquest of Canaan, for he put into Noah's mouth the words:

> Cursed be Canaan—the lowest of slaves shall he be to his brothers. Blessed be the Lord, the God of Shem—let Canaan be a slave to them . . . . May God enlarge Japheth, and let him dwell in the tents of Shem, and let Canaan be a slave to them. [9]

What this passage does show is that 2,500 years ago, man was invoking sacred scripture in order to defend his actions. However, the "curse of Ham" has nothing whatsoever to do with Negroes! A more relevant reference to blacks in the Bible can be found in *Amos:* 9:7, where it is written that God through the prophet, warned the Israelites to expect no special favors from Him because of their ethnic identity:

> Are ye not as the children of the Ethiopians unto Me, O children of Israel? saith the Lord.

The Lord is God of all mankind: blacks are just as much His children as are Jews!

That racist doctrine cannot be supported by evidence is a fact of tremendous importance: for *if* there is nothing *inherently* inferior about the Negro race, if Negroes do *not* differ significantly from whites in their innate capacity for intelligence, will power or crime, then the explanation for their behavior *must* be found in the conditions which they have experienced. The question then becomes: *Which* conditions can account for the apparent inability of most Negroes to enter the mainstream of American life?

The Unique Experiences of the American Negro

"If we Jews could make it, why can't they?" Such a statement implies that the experiences of Jews and Negroes have been much the same, both having suffered from poverty and prejudice. The fact is that the conditions encountered by the Jewish immigrant were vastly different from those which today confront the Negro. A comparison of the experiences of the two groups will help us understand the uniqueness of the Negro's position in American life.

1. The Lack of a Literate and Commercial Heritage

When the Jews were allowed to enter the modern world, their community was the end-product of three thousand years of a *literate and commercial civilization.* In marked contrast, the American Negro is the end-product of a slave society, which made it almost impossible for its members to become literate, skilled, and knowledgeable in the ways of the modern world.

When Jewish immigrants were admitted to the United States in the early twentieth century, their most common occupations were listed as tailor, clerk, shoemaker, merchant, dressmaker, and butcher. They were accustomed to the ways of the business world, and their skills could immediately be put to use in an America of expanding opportunity. However, when the Negro was forcibly brought to America from Africa, he had no such training in the arts of Western civilization. As a slave, he was given no opportunity for such training, and after the Civil War, the segregated and unequal school system served effectively to keep him in his place, namely, all but illiterate and low man on the economic totem pole.

The slum child of today is the inheritor of this under-developed culture. His parents rarely have the kind of skills that would enable them to hold anything other than menial jobs: maid, janitor, handyman. Since so many of these parents have emerged from a system that stifled their cultural development, their homes are often without books or newspapers. Reading, therefore, is something their children may do only in the classroom. It was reported that half of one group of such children lived in homes where there were no pencils! Conversation in such homes is usually abrupt, consisting primarily of phrases rather than sentences. (Compare this with the "talky-ness" of many a Jewish home.) Consequently, the vocabulary of the Negro lower-class child will be far less than that of a middle-class child. Also, because of crowded living conditions, he will probably be unable to find a quiet place to do his homework. Little wonder that the reading level in his school is far below the average.[10]

The point is that, largely because of yesterday's slavery and today's slums, the Negro child (unlike the Jewish child of immigrant parents) lacks a heritage of those basic skills so essential to becoming really a part of American life.

Discussion: Why did most Jewish immigrants have some kind of a trade or business? What role did the Jews of Europe play in the economy of their respective countries? How did discrimination against the Jewish people, in some way, help equip them for participation in mercantile and capitalist societies?

2. Problems of "Moving Up" in Today's World

The German Jewish immigrants who came to the United States in the middle of the nineteenth century and the Eastern European Jews who fled Czarist persecution from 1880 to 1914 were both fortunate to find an America of abundant opportunity. As the nation moved westward, merchants were needed to bring the products of the industrial East to the new frontiers, and many German Jews were admirably equipped by their cultural background to become part of this expanding commercial scene. Some years later when Russian and Polish Jews poured into the cities on the Eastern seaboard, their horizons were more limited. Still, they could (and did) go to work for German Jewish clothing manufacturers, and it was not too difficult for a man, after accumulating a little capital, to go into business for himself. Then, too, there was a great need for *unskilled* labor. In those days, even a peddler could make a living!

Today, when the Negro is attempting to move upward on the economic ladder, he finds certain obstacles not encountered by former generations, at least, to the same degree.

a. *Automation:* Bayard Rustin has written:

. . . We live in a society where, as Secretary of Labor, Willard Wirtz puts it, machines have the equivalent of a high school diploma. Yet the average educational attainment of American Negroes is 8.2 years.11

The hypothesis that the labor-saving mechanization of the economy is making it much more difficult for unskilled workers to find jobs is currently being debated by social scientists. It is generally agreed that the proportion of unskilled and semi-skilled workers to the total work force is decreasing and will continue to do so. However, the absolute

[65]

number of such "blue-collar workers" is increasing.[12] The question is: Are the number of jobs available for the unskilled sufficient to take care of the dramatic increase in the size of the labor force due to the postwar baby boom and the growing desire of women to work? Thousands of our young people and many of our women are simply not equipped to hold jobs that require specialized training, and those who are equipped may displace others who are less skilled.

A careful economist, Robert Heilbroner, has explained that we do not have enough statistics to be certain of the effects of automation. He did advance the suggestion that the uniqueness of today's problem is that the "service sector" of our economy is for the first time seriously affected by mechanization: Gone are the days when there was a pin-boy behind every bowling alley! In the past, workers who, because of automation, were not needed in the farm or factory, tended to go into service occupations. However, now that automation is taking place from the laundromat to the carwash, where will the displaced workers go? "There is now no expansive market sector left."[13]

So, it is possible that automation may be a greater problem for today's unskilled worker than for the unskilled of previous generations for two reasons: the enlarged labor force and the more pervasive presence of mechanization throughout the entire economy.

b. *Big Business and Mobility:* A major reason for the rapid rise of many Jewish immigrants was that, in earlier decades, the world of business offered tremendous opportunity even for the man of very modest means. Today, with the advent of giant chain stores that offer more goods at lower prices, the "small businessman" confronts problems never faced by his counterpart several decades ago. (A sensitive portrayal of one such man who found the changed conditions too much for him is Bernard Malamud's picture of the grocer Morris Bober in *The Assistant.*) Of course, thousands of merchants make good livings in modest stores, but, as most of them will tell you, it is no longer so easy to start on a shoestring and build up a substantial business.

There are surely other ways of climbing the economic ladder—the professions, science, government, academics, management— but these areas require considerably more education than our Jewish immigrants had when they rose from poverty. The Negro slum dweller must begin his climb so far behind that he might understandably wonder: What's the use of trying? Compare him with the immigrant who could go into business for himself without anyone asking him if he had a college degree.

It may be impossible to measure precisely the quantity of opportunity offered young Americans. For the culturally advantaged that opportunity is surely great. But for a group that is in the latter half of the twentieth century attempting to break into the American mainstream, the cumulative effect of new conditions can be overwhelming: the youth boom, working women, automation in *all* sectors of the economy, the competition of bigness and the requirement of a higher education before one can even begin the climb. This may be what Bayard Rustin meant when he wrote ". . . an individual will no longer be able to start at the bottom and work his way up; he will have to start in the middle or top and hold on tight."[14]

Discussion: Employers have pointed out that when jobs requiring no special skills *are* available, slum dwellers do not even want them. This "unwillingness to work" is often ascribed to high welfare payments: Why should he work when he can make almost as much money drawing checks from the government? The implication may be that only if welfare payments were cut, more slum dwellers would go to work.

Social workers respond that there are more cases of men seeking jobs than of jobs "seeking" men. They strongly protest a decrease in welfare payments, which at their present level do not always provide for the basic necessities of life. What is really needed is a higher minimum wage, so that the unskilled worker will have more incentive for working. What is your opinion?

In the light of the previous section, compare the opportunities for advancement open to the man without a high school diploma in previous generations and the opportunities open to such a man today.

Is it possible that in years past uneducated workers might have been more willing to work because they could see a future for themselves, despite their lack of formal education?

3. The Effect of Slavery and Slums on the Negro Family

The Jewish people emerged from the ghetto with their family life intact. Despite all the persecution in the late Middle Ages, the Jews were allowed to run their own community affairs and to preserve their basic institutions, and there was none more basic than the family. It was in the home that the Jewish child received the warmth and love that insulated him against the coldness of an often hostile world. The Jewish child emerged from his home with a sense of his own worth and a belief in his own capacity to make the most of his life.

On the other hand, the Negro's family life was shattered by slavery. Fathers, mothers, and children were separated according to the whim of the slave-marketeers. The Jim Crow System, which emerged from the Reconstruction era, hardly encouraged the development of a stable family life. Deprived of his vote, called "boy" by men half his age, educated to be a sharecropper, the Negro father was in no position to be an encouraging model for his son. To escape such stifling conditions, thousands of Southern Negroes migrated to Northern cities where they found not "the promised land" but crowded tenements and unemployment. Again, the father was usually unable to provide strength and security. According to the Moynihan Report, published in 1965 by the Department of Labor, one Negro family in four is fatherless. "It has been estimated that only a minority of Negro children reach the age of 18 having lived all their lives with both their parents."[15] In central Harlem only half the children live with both father and mother.

What happens to the children of a community when family life is so shattered? With mother at work and father either ineffective or absent, the child has little guidance, so he turns to the street. It is not unusual to hear such parents say of their five-year-old child: "We can't do a thing with

[68]

him." By the age of ten, the street has often taken over and parental authority is nil. Without a secure home environment, a child will have great difficulty in developing a sense of his own worth. Given the instability of so many Negro families, it was hardly surprising that a study conducted by the Institute for Developmental Studies at New York Medical College re- ported that while 30 percent of white slum children felt inferior to other children, fully *80 percent* of Negro children had inferiority feeling.[16]

When family life is so unstable that children are without parental guidance and self-respect, then such children will not have an equal chance in either the academic or economic rat race.

Discussion: The "Moynihan Report" that brought public attention to the problems of the disadvantaged Negro family has been criticized by some as giving encouragement to bigots. How could an analysis that revealed the instability of some Negro families give any support to racists? How do you think Moynihan answered such a charge? (See the *American Jewish Year Book,* 1966, p. 100.)

What role did Judaism, as a religion, play in strengthening the bonds of Jewish family life? Do you agree with the following state- ment: "It is both futile and condescending to hold up to Negroes the example of the Jewish home"?

4. Racial Discrimination Is Different

The American Jew has known the meaning of discrimination. He has known firms that would not employ him, colleges that would not admit him, and clubs that barred him from membership. However, even during the Depression when anti- Semitism was at its height, the overwhelming majority of American Jews were not significantly affected by discrimi- nating employers. Their children *were* able to secure a higher education. The bigotry they encountered was as of nothing compared with the barriers that have confronted the American Negro.

a. Employment

Thus far Negro unemployment has been explained as a result of the lack of a literate and commercial heritage, the lack of opportunity more readily available to early generations of immigrants and the lack of a stable family life. However, it is all too clear that even when Negroes do secure the training and develop the ability to earn a decent living, they may not be given the same opportunity as whites with comparable qualifications.

There is no question but that for decades American Negroes have been discriminated against by both employers and labor unions. In 1962, the unemployment rate among Negro craftsmen, foremen, and clerical workers was about twice as high as the rate among whites who had similar skills.[17] Herman Miller, in 1964, reported that Negro college graduates can expect to earn in their lifetime only as much as whites who have not gone beyond the eighth grade. But did not the Civil Rights Act of 1964 with its Equal Employment Opportunity Commission change all that? Yes and No.

According to Franklin D. Roosevelt, Jr., chairman of the commission, "Walls are literally coming down . . . . Most employers are out-reaching individual complaints to open up new opportunities for minorities in their plants and businesses." Still, such deep-rooted patterns do not disappear overnight. From July 2 to December 31, 1965, the commission charged 1,822 employers and 466 unions with discrimination.[18] This, of course, does not include the hundreds of cases brought before state and municipal agencies. Further evidence of continued unequal treatment is to be found in the fact that the national unemployment rate of Negro high school *graduates* (16 to 21 years old) was, in 1965, 15 percent—about 2 percentage points higher than the jobless rate for white high school *dropouts.*[19]

So, while walls may be coming down, some are crumbling more quickly than others. In addition to employers who do not wish to comply with the fair employment standards, there are others who unintentionally have set up job criteria that exclude Negroes. For example, a high school diploma may be required even though "dropouts" may very well have the ability needed for the particular task. Tests, used to eliminate incompetents, have frequently been found to measure academic achievements not needed on the job. Consequently, the commission has issued "guidelines on employment testing procedures."

Another wall that has not been completely leveled may still be encountered in some unions. While the large industrial unions were among the first to eliminate discrimination, certain craft unions have been very slow to accept Negroes into their apprentice programs. According to one Urban League employment specialist, Negroes continue to find it difficult if not impossible to join the unions of machinists, electrical workers, tool and dye makers, lithographers, and stone-masons. The construction industry and the plumbers are, as a result of pressures from Washington, showing some signs of a more open policy.

As more opportunities for Negroes gradually appear, there is often a shortage of qualified applicants. This should hardly be a surprise. A community that has for three hundred years been cut off from employment requiring skill and advanced education cannot be expected suddenly to produce young people with such training. Not only does the schooling, itself, take time, but it is far from easy to convince parents so accustomed to racial barriers, that there are, for their children, real openings in the walls. A common attitude is still that of the parents of Claude Brown who somehow managed to break out of Harlem and write a book about his escape. Claude's father just did not see the need for "all that education," and his mother kept warning him: "Don't you go wanting things not for you."[20]

While it is true that discrimination in employment opportunities is finally on the decrease for the American Negro, it is also true that he is still shut out by doors that were never closed to American Jews. Negro parents and children must now be convinced that enough doors are open (and are opening) so that their striving will be worthwhile.

b. Education

The inadequate education of the Negro slum child is

usually ascribed to his culturally deprived background. Certainly the lack of a literate heritage and the shattering of so many Negro families are major reasons for the low academic standards of slum schools. However, these are not the only reasons.

James Conant, in *Slums and Suburbs,* reported that in 1961 the expenditure per pupil in suburban schools often ran as high as $1,000 for the year. The expenditure per pupil in the slum school was usually less than $500. Suburban schools would often have a staff of 70 for every 1,000 pupils. A slum school, where *more* attention to individuals is needed, would usually have a staff of 40 per 1,000 students.[21] Charles Silberman has noted that in Chicago, according to a 1961 Civil Rights Commission report, appropriations per pupil averaged 21 percent less in all Negro schools than in all white schools. When integrated schools became predominantly Negro, suddenly there were shortages of texts, a loss of specialists, and an increase in substitute teachers. Kenneth Clark has maintained that despite all the problems of the Negro child, he could learn much more readily, *if he were being taught effectively.*[22] Clark's charge is that too many slum school teachers do not believe that their children have the ability to learn. The children naturally adopt their teacher's attitude—that they are unteachable—and then, of course, they do not learn!

Residential segregation forces Negro children to attend schools that are predominantly Negro. This is called "de facto segregation," which to James Baldwin means that "Negroes are segregated, but nobody did it."[23] The United States Commission on Civil Rights in 1967 came to the conclusion that Negro children in majority-Negro schools will not learn as rapidly as similar Negro children in majority-white schools. However, the implication of this conclusion that there should be more rapid integration has been considered impractical by some civil rights leaders who insist that segregated children can still, with sufficient compensatory help, be well educated. Many white parents consider integration to be, in some sense, harmful. The arguments on all sides of this debate will be explored in the following chapter.

For our present purposes, we would summarize those factors making for unequal educational opportunity for Negro children who live in the slums as: (1) lack of a literate heritage; (2) frequent family instability; (3) less funds available for lower-class schools; (4) poorer quality of education: inadequate facilities, crowded classrooms, less competent teaching; (5) the effect of racial isolation.

c. Housing

A clear picture of Negro housing in the slum has been painted by Lenora Berson in her study of the story behind the Philadelphia riot of 1964.[24] In the North Side ghetto, most of the homes had been built between 1850 and 1900; 53 percent of the dwellings were substandard, meaning, for example, staircases without bannisters, exposed wiring or faulty plumbing. Because of the run-down condition of the buildings, the landlords thought it too costly to make repairs, unless they were forced to do so by the commissioner of Licenses and Inspection. It was found that out of 391 violations of the Housing Code, only *eight* were attributed by the commissioner to the tenants, themselves. One can understand why Negroes become infuriated when middle-class whites advise them to take better care of their landlord's property.

It is common knowledge that Negroes in the great urban centers often find it impossible to buy homes outside of the ghetto. A few middle-class business or professional people do manage to escape. However, the vast majority must remain within the invisible wall. So the crowding becomes even more unbearable: Seven living in one room is not unusual. In Harlem, in the early 1960's 232,792 people were crammed into the area of three and one-half square miles.[25]

Berson reported that Philadelphia slum dwellers had to pay about 35 percent of their income for rent, although 20-25 percent was the figure recommended by the Department of Labor. So high was the rent that a mother with three children drawing a welfare check was left, after paying the landlord, with $27.15 per week for food, clothing, and all other expenses, that is, one-third less than was needed for minimum daily subsistence according to the government. In Pennsylvania, as well as in other states of our prosperous nation, it is a shocking fact that welfare payments do not provide enough money for some families to secure adequate food, clothing, and shelter!

Discussion: What appears as "discrimination" from the viewpoint of the victim and the government is usually justified by arguments based on economic necessity. For example, officials of those craft unions accused of discrimination insist that they do *not* exclude Negroes because they are Negroes. For the union to secure advantages for its members, their number must be limited; otherwise there would be less work for everybody. Naturally, members choose to offer what openings there are to those bound to them by friendship or family ties. The government, on the other hand, considers the right to equal opportunity to make a living to be more basic than the right to pass on one's union membership to one's family and friends. What is your opinion?

The dramatic difference between slum and suburban school environments has been minimized by the Coleman Report (U.S. Dept. of HEW) which in 1966, compared school conditions of Negroes and whites *throughout the nation.* Since most white Americans do not live in suburban communities that can afford a high quality of education, the report found that the differences between black and white school environments were, on the average, not so great as had been imagined. This implies that differences in achievements of black and white children are due more to non-school factors in slum living than to the school environment, itself. The question remains: *should* some schools have more adequate facilities, smaller class size and more experienced teachers than others? If so, should the better conditions be provided for children in the slums or for those in the suburbs?

The Voice of the Ghetto

In this chapter we have been examining historical forces and sociological conditions in an effort to understand some of the reasons why so many Negroes have been unable to escape the mire of poverty. We have explored their lack of a literate and commercial background; the special problems of moving up in today's world of exploding population and automation; the effect of slavery and slums on the Negro family; discrimination in employment, education, and housing.

However, the slum dweller himself does not think in terms of forces or conditions or statistical studies. He sees himself trapped in the dark ghetto while all around him the bright lights of the affluent society shine brightly, telling him that everyone else is enjoying the good life. Television commercials taunt him with impossible dreams: "Wouldn't you really rather have a Buick!" Little wonder that when he saves a few dollars he may well buy some extravagant symbol of the world that beckons but will not admit him. He may not be able to explain all the social and historical reasons why he cannot escape his slum, but, seeing prosperity all around the ghetto, he is enraged that he should be excluded from the inviting American dream.

If we would try to understand what gives the Negro pain, we should—after reading all the statistics—listen to his voice:

> It may sound funny to you but I often wake up at night from a dream in which I've at last got a union card.26
> Young man, age 20

> A lot of times, when I'm working I become as despondent as hell and I feel like crying. I'm not a man, none of us are men! I don't own anything.27   Man, age 30

> The way the Man has us, he has us wanting to kill one another. Dog eat dog, amongst us! He has us, like we're so hungry up here, he has us so tight! Like his rent is due, my rent is due. It's Friday. The Man wants sixty-five dollars. If you are three days over, or don't have the money; like that, he wants to give you a dispossess 28   Man, age 31

Claude Brown, as a child in Harlem, learned first that fighting was the only way to gain self-respect in the streets. Then he realized that fighting would eventually lead to knifing . . . and maybe dying . . . .

> . . . if you were going to be respected in Harlem, you had to be a bad nigger; and if you were going to be a bad nigger, you had to be ready to die. I wasn't ready to do any of that stuff, but I had to . . . there was no place to go, and it seemed like all life was just closing in on me and squashing me to death.29

[75]

James Baldwin, the angry poet of the revolution, expressed with candor the feeling of his people:

> You were born where you were born and faced the future that you faced because you were black and *for no other reason.* You were born into a society which spelled out, with brutal clarity, and in as many ways as possible, that you were a worthless human being.30

> To be a Negro in this country and to be relatively conscious is to be in a rage almost all the time.31

On Delinquency and Riots

Having become aware of the conditions, past and present, that have led to the accumulation of such frustration, we may now be better able to understand the high rate of delinquency in the dark ghetto. According to the Uniform Crime Reports, while Negroes in 1960 composed only one-tenth of the population, they constituted nearly one-third of those persons arrested for all offenses. The main cause of such racial imbalance should by now be clear. Marvin Wolfgang, in *Crime and Race,* has suggested an explanation, which should make sense in the light of our discussion thus far: Delinquency is "a protest against the social system that blocks the path to success" as well as "a way albeit illegitimate, to acquire recognition and status" within the deprived group:

> Difficult to find are the legitimate opportunities to success (education, good job, proper contacts); far more accessible are the illegitimate opportunities (theft, gambling, drugs) to obtain the symbols of success (car, property, power).32

Louis Lomax has written that Negroes commit crimes for three main reasons: (1) the need for money for basic necessities; (2) the need to escape the frustrating reality of ghetto life; (3) the desire to "get back" at the white man.33

As for the summer riots, which annually shock the country, to psychologist Kenneth Clark, "the wonder is there have been so few."34 Given the desperation of human beings who see no way out of their predicament, we might expect their anger to build until it bursts into flame. To state this in more precise terms: "The central fact about a race riot is that it represents an explosion of feeling arising from a festering discontent that could find no other, more acceptable avenue of expression and communication."[35]

These explosions have usually been set off by incidents involving the police. Most Negroes in the ghetto are convinced that the purpose of the police is to protect white people. From January through July, 1964, five Negro women were assaulted in one block in the Philadelphia ghetto. No one was arrested. Whatever degree of truth there is in the charges of bias and brutality, the basic reason for the Negro's distrust of the police was pointed out by Bayard Rustin: They are the protectors of what is to the slum dweller an unjust order; therefore, they are natural targets for bitter anger directed against that order.[36]

Slum merchants are also obvious targets for Negro frustration. To angry Negroes these businessmen often appear as parasites who are sending their children to college on the money squeezed out of the slum. Since in many ghettos, a large portion of the merchants are Jewish, Negro anti-Semitism has become increasingly evident. How widespread is this phenomenon? What are its causes? How might Jews respond? These questions will be discussed in Chapter Six.

A report of the President's Commission on Law Enforcement and the Administration of Justice concluded in February, 1967, that riots, although exploited by agitators, were spontaneous outbursts of "a more or less representative cross section of the Negro community, particularly its young men, many of whom had lived in the neighborhood for many years and were steadily unemployed." The uprisings were deliberate in the sense that they were directed against those specific institutions that the participants thought of as being their principal oppressors: the police, white passers-by, white-owned businesses, especially those felt to be exploiting the customers, and loan offices. "Homes, schools, churches, and libraries were, by and large, left alone." In a UCLA study of violence in Watts, 55 percent of the Negroes interviewed felt that one result of the explosion would be to *diminish* racial problems by forcing the white community to recognize the need to eliminate the conditions that give rise to riots. [37]

In February, 1968, the President's Commission on Civil Disorder, led by Governor Otto Kerner of Illinois, concluded that "white racism is essentially responsible for the explosive mixture which has been accumulating in our cities since the end of World War II."* The report, based on an intensive analysis of the disorders in ten cities including Newark, Detroit, and Atlanta, found that contrary to the 1967 Commission's conclusion, the typical rioter was not *un*employed but *under*employed or employed in a menial job. A supplementary report issued in July, 1968, that took into account riots in Cincinnati, Dayton, Grand Rapids, and New Haven, confirmed this finding by stating that three-fourths of those arrested *were* employed. Evidently young men working part-time at menial dead-end jobs are the angriest and most frustrated in the ghetto, a thought that gives added significance to the high rate of subemployment discussed in Chapter Two. The July report also found that, contrary to the popular notion, criminals were not overrepresented among the arrestees in proportion to the neighborhood population. Also, the number of outsiders from other communities was extremely small, only one percent. This study did confirm the 1967 finding that most residents, while disapproving of violence, did believe that "the riots have beneficial consequences by increasing white society's concern to improve the Negro's condition." [38]

The explosion in Detroit (July, 1967) provided the clearest evidence of the role of organized revolutionaries. Louis Lomax has reported how, before the riot, "magazine salesmen" went from door to door soliciting support for violence and intimidating those who protested their tactics. The outburst was, at first, spontaneous, triggered by a police raid on an after-hours club that the neighbors had been com-

---

*See Appendix Six for excerpts from the findings of the President's Commission on Civil Disorder, 1968. Also see Murray Friedman, "Is White Racism the Problem?" *Commentary*, Vol. 47:I, Jan., 1969.

plaining about for months. Negro leaders, thinking they understood their people, advised the police commissioner to keep his men in check so that the unorganized disorder would run its course. They did not reckon with the "professionals" who moved methodically from block to block smashing windows and encouraging looters, nor did they take into account the snipers who were organized to do their job with the precision of guerilla warfare. That Detroit was more of a "class riot" than a race riot was suggested by the violence in middle-class Negro neighborhoods, by the threats of revolutionaries against the "rich niggers," and by evidence hinting at the *possible* involvement of some whites in the uprising. [39]

Whatever the role of instigators may be, they can hardly be considered the fundamental cause of civil disorder. It is obvious that no revolutionary clique can, by itself, cause a riot. Such eruptions of hatred take place only when the mass frustration is at a breaking point. The demagogue is only effective when the people are in a mood to listen. The conditions that create such a mood are, therefore, the most significant reasons for the riots. In a sense, the extremists, themselves, are the products of those conditions.*

Discussion: "If Claude Brown could make it, why can't the rest of them?" In his remarkable autobiography, Brown vividly describes the life of violence, narcotics, and prostitution that has dragged so many Harlem Negroes down into the depths of hopelessness but that somehow he managed to overcome. The fact that a few slumdwellers, because of either exceptional inner strength or the chance contact with a truly concerned human being who knew how to awaken potential, have managed to rise above the quicksand of slum life—this fact somehow may become an argument that if *one* could do it, they *all* should be able to escape.

What is the fallacy of this argument? Some of the Jews of

---

*See Appendix Six for excerpts from the findings of the President's Commission on Civil Disorder, 1968.

Europe survived the death-camps because of exceptional strength or chance contact with benevolent non-Jews or just plain luck. Could the persecution of the Jews ever be justified by the argument that "some made it"?

Consider a typical kindergarten class in an all-white suburb. Imagine that the entire class was suddenly placed in a slum school and adopted by families living in the slum neighborhood. How many students do you think would be able to overcome the disadvantages of their new life?

On Understanding and Judging

In this chapter we have attempted to understand something of the conditions Negroes have experienced in America. Once these conditions are understood, then the responsibility for the Negro poor is shifted from traits which are allegedly ingrained in the Negro character to the very real web of social and economic injustice in which he finds himself caught.

There are some people who confuse *understanding* behavior with *excusing* or *justifying* such behavior. There need be no such confusion. One may still condemn a crime and at the same time attempt to understand why the criminal feels compelled to commit it. In fact, if one's basic interest is the elimination of such criminal behavior, then he should do all he can to eliminate the conditions that tend to produce it.

How should one feel about the criminal himself? Hillel gave an interesting response to this question: "Do not judge your neighbor until you have come into his place."[40] It is ultimately impossible for a white person to put himself in the place of a Negro slum dweller. We cannot know how we would be acting were we viewing the world from the streets of Harlem. Since we can never be exactly in his place, since we cannot know what we might be doing, were we caught in the quicksand of slum life, then Hillel's conclusion would seem to be: Do not judge your neighbor. Let God do whatever condemning has to be done.

It is for us not to condemn others but to make certain that we are living up to our own responsibilities. In this spirit, we would now raise the crucial question: How can we speedily eradicate those conditions which breed poverty and prejudice, frustration, and violence? In the next chapter we shall examine the specific proposals that have been made in order to bring the Negro into the mainstream of American life.

Chapter Five

INTO THE MAINSTREAM

> ... Freedom is not enough. You do not wipe away the scars
> of centuries by saying: Now you are free to go where you
> want, or do as you desire, and choose the leaders you please.
> You do not take a person who, for years, has been hobbled
> by chains and liberate him, bring him up to the starting line of
> a race and then say, "You are free to compete with all the
> others" and still justly believe that you have been completely
> fair. Thus it is not enough just to open the gates of opportunity.
> All our citizens must have the ability to walk through those
> gates.

Thus did President Lyndon Johnson, speaking in June, 1965,
at Howard University, sum up the situation of thousands of
American Negroes.

Many of the chains *are* off. Segregation can no longer
be enforced by state and local governments. Discrimination
in employment and intimidation at the ballot box have been
outlawed by civil rights acts. However, it is no easy matter
for anyone to overcome the effects of being chained for three
hundred years. One may tell the child of the ghetto that the
sky is the limit, but he must still find some way to escape
the quicksand of slum life, where families are unstable, schools
are inferior, and theft, prostitution, and narcotics are accepted
as part of the normal way of life. No one growing up in such a
world has, in fact, the same chance in the highly competitive
pursuit of happiness as have other Americans. The President
recognized this when he said that it is just not fair to take the
chains off and say: Run the race.

This same idea was more colorfully if less delicately
phrased by an angry young Negro, quoted in *Life* magazine:

> Equal opportunity, my sweet obscenity. The way these kids
> see it, equality is like Whitey holds you by the belt at the
> starting line until everyone else is halfway around the track,

then gives you a big slap on the rump and says, "Go, baby, you're equal!"[1]

Clearly something more must be done if the equality in theory is to become equality in fact. In this chapter we shall discuss three proposals intended to bring more Negroes into the mainstream of American life:

1.) compensatory programs designed to give disadvantaged Negroes (and/or whites) real equality of opportunity;
2.) open occupancy as the law of the land;
3.) special techniques to hasten integration in the schools.

1. Compensatory Programs

Sometimes termed "preferential treatment," such programs are attempts to compensate slumdwellers for the disadvantages they suffer as a result of conditions beyond their control. Some proposals provide special treatment specifically for the Negro, for example, quota hiring and the "Marshall Plan." Others would favor the poor in general: for example, the War against Poverty and the Freedom Budget.

    a. *"Quota Hiring."* In the early sixties, the four hundred ministers of Philadelphia insisted that certain firms which, in their view, had a history of discrimination should hire a specified number of Negroes for particular kinds of jobs before a given date. If a firm did not cooperate, the ministers would urge the Negroes of Philadelphia not to purchase its product. So effective was this technique that Gulf Oil and Sun Oil eventually gave in to the demands, and Pepsi-Cola and Esso capitulated before the boycott was actually called.

    This technique has been branded as "racism in reverse," and its critics argue as follows: If X number of Negroes must be hired in Y number of months, this will inevitably mean that some whites who are better qualified for the positions will be passed over, and discrimination against whites today is just as unfair as was bias against Negroes yesterday.

In defense of such preferential hiring, Charles Silberman has contended that, unless a conscious attempt is made to hire Negroes *as Negroes,* many firms will never change their inequitable practices! Those in charge of personnel can always find reasons for rejecting *qualified* Negro applicants. So, practically speaking, the only way to break down the barrier is by making it a matter of policy to employ a certain number of Negroes. According to this view, it is unfortunate that some deserving whites are treated unfairly, but such is the price that must be paid if Negroes are ever to achieve the fact of equality.[2]

Discussion: One important reason that Jewish immigrants were able to make their way into the mainstream of American life was that the Jews, as did other immigrant groups, "took care of their own." This meant that Jewish employers made it a point to hire Jewish employees even though non-Jews equally or more qualified for the job were available. Today there are not enough Negro employers to provide a similar service for "their own."

What is your opinion of the strategy of the four hundred ministers? Were Jewish employers in decades past justified in favoring their fellow Jews?*

b. *The Marshall Plan.* In the early 1960's Whitney Young, Jr., was advocating that the Negroes be certified as an underdeveloped people within America. Just as the European nations after World War II required a Marshall Plan to revive their economic life, so the American Negro community, victimized by slavery and slums, requires a massive expenditure of funds if it is to assume its proper place in American life. In Mr. Young's words:

For nearly four hundred years the Negro has been consciously and deliberately excluded (from the American mainstream). During this time he has been denied even the barest minimum in health, education, housing, and cultural outlets. For him to

---

*See Opinionaire Item 17.

catch up will require a few years of *deliberate inclusion* and *special programming* within the integrated framework to offset the scars which were inevitable under the kind of environment which America subjected him to. There is no way for the back wheels of a car to catch up with the front wheels even though they are going at the same rate of speed unless something special happens.3

That society has an obligation to do "something special" for its victims is reminiscent of the rabbinic doctrine of, *teshuvah shelemah,* complete repentance. According to our tradition, one should not only feel remorse over his sins. To earn *complete* repentance, he must compensate the person sinned against for whatever harm was done him.

In May, 1969, the National Black Economic Development Conference adopted James Forman's "Black Manifesto," which demanded of churches and synagogues 500 million dollars in reparations: religious institutions should pay because their membership has exploited and continues to exploit black people. Forman's methods (disrupting church services) and his revolutionary goal of destroying capitalism have been widely criticized, but certain basic questions remain:

> Does white society owe compensation to those it has victimized? If so, are religious institutions morally in debt? Can the synagogue be considered responsible for racist policies in America?

c. *War Against Poverty.* The government's anti-poverty program is based on special treatment for the poor of all races. (See Chapter Two.) Critics of existing programs range from those who claim that too much has already been done to those who charge "tokenism."

The "classical liberal" will usually maintain that as long as people are equal under the law, they simply have to take their chances in the game of life. Some will win, others will lose. The losers may be the object of our charity, but society has no obligation to give them favored treatment because they lost the race. Indeed, one of the incentives in the capitalist system is the discomfort of losing. The "modern" or "welfare" liberal maintains that the poor are not primarily responsible for their plight. People are poor for all kinds of reasons that have nothing to do with innate ability. Poverty can be inherited, just as can wealth. The child raised in the slum could hardly be held responsible for not overcoming the tremendous obstacles never dreamed of by middle-class children. Therefore, society owes the children of poverty (whatever their age or race) not condescending charity but the means to live in dignity and to develop whatever potential they may have. Of those who accept the modern liberal position, an increasing number are supporting what the A. Philip Randolph Institute has titled, "A Freedom Budget for All Americans."

d. *The Freedom Budget.* In September, 1966, Randolph together with an impressive group of economists and social scientists proposed that over a ten-year period the federal government spends annually an average of 18.5 billion dollars *more* than was spent in 1965, for the attainment of full employment and the liquidation of poverty. This 185 billion dollars would (according to proponents of the Freedom Budget) come from America's "economic growth dividend." That is to say, if we put all our resources to work, the country's production would rise over the next ten years an average of $244 billion per year. At the present tax rate, the government would receive an average of $10 billion per year in additional taxes. This would mean $400 billion more that would be available for spending over the next ten years, simply as a result of America's increasing productive power. From these revenues, the advocates of the Freedom Budget propose to spend $185 billion to meet the nation's critical needs.[4] Since, according to this view, our nation *can* afford the cost of such a massive attack on poverty without significantly lowering anyone's standard of living, the issue— say the advocates—is no longer *economic* but *moral* in nature. Specifically, should we use the increasing productive power of our nation to enable the haves to gain even more goods and services than they now possess, or should we devote the increase in our productive power to raising the have-nots out of poverty?

Even though proponents of the Freedom Budget maintain that America can, with no substantial self-sacrifice, eliminate poverty, still as long as this nation is engaged in war, the question of priority will be a serious one. Rev. Martin Luther King has dealt with this question by pointing out that we are spending a half million dollars to kill every enemy soldier in Vietnam, and only fifty-three dollars annually to aid every impoverished American.[5] The Freedom Budget would require but a fraction of what is spent each year in Vietnam, and its advocates argue that the well-being of the American poor should matter at least as much to our nation's leaders as does the welfare of the Vietnamese peasants.

Among the proposals of this massive attack on poverty are the following:[*]

1.) Raise the minimum wage, thus lifting many out of poverty and increasing the demand for goods and the number of workers needed to meet that demand.

2.) Guarantee a level of income above the poverty level for all those who legitimately cannot obtain it through their own efforts, thus bringing out of poverty 40 percent of the poor who cannot or should not work because of age or other disabling factors.

3.) Provide a decent home for every American family, through government aid to private builders and larger Urban Renewal programs.

4.) Provide adequate educational opportunities by, among other means, building one hundred thousand new classrooms and training one hundred thousand new teachers each year, and developing further the compensatory programs for the culturally disadvantaged.[6]

Discussion: 1. *The Freedom Budget and Vietnam:* With periodic demands for higher taxes to meet the needs of the war in Vietnam, can we really afford the Freedom Budget? Which is more vital to America's interest: That the communists be prevented from having a dominant voice in South Vietnam or that poverty be eliminated in America? Should civil rights leaders criticize the American involvement in Viet-

---

*Compare these recommendations with those of the 1968 Commission on Civil Disorders. See Appendix VI.

nam? Could Martin Luther King, as a believer in nonviolence, be consistent and not criticize that involvement?

2. *Obligations to the Poor:* What would be the classical liberal's objection to the Freedom Budget? If the "losers" in the economic race are guaranteed an annual income above the poverty level, do you think that most of them would stop trying to "get ahead"? If you were given such a minimal income, would you retire?

3. *Problem of Inflation:* Some have claimed that the Freedom Budget, if enacted, would lead to inflation since a high demand for goods and services would mean higher prices, and so the poor would not really be helped. Proponents respond that so long as we are not doing more than our resources permit there is no serious problem, and if one should develop, the government can meet it without penalizing the poor. Those interested in pursuing this discussion might read: *Freedom Budget* pamphlet, pp. 71-75.

Poverty in Jewish Tradition

In an interesting discussion of the Jewish attitude towards poverty, Rabbi Richard Hirsch makes clear that as early as the second century, the rabbis had developed laws and institutions designed to meet the basic needs of the poor.[7] In the *Kuppah* ("box"), enough funds were collected to provide for the *local* poor. A second fund, called *Tamchui,* or "bowl," made possible daily distribution of food not only to residents but to transients as well. In the *Mishnah* detailed laws spell out just who is to receive how much:

> A poor man that is journeying from place to place should be given not less than one loaf worth a *pondion* (from wheat costing) one *sela* for four *seahs* . . . . If he stays over the Sabbath he should be given food enough for three meals. If a man has food enough for two meals he may not take aught from the *Tamchui,* and if enough for fourteen meals he may not take aught from the *Kuppah* . . . . If a man had two hundred zuz, he may not take (charity) . . . if he had hundred less one *denar,* and even a thousand (householders) together gave him each (one *denar*), he may take . . . .[8]

By the Middle Ages, the Jewish community was regulating market prices so that the needy could buy food and other commodities at cost. In some areas, there was even "rent control," so that the poor could be given housing at rates they could afford.9

To those who might become impatient with the less fortunate, our tradition has a clear response:

> If your brother be waxen poor, you shall not suffer him to fall. He is like a load resting on a wall; one man can then hold it, and prevent it from falling, but if it has once fallen to the ground, five men cannot raise it up again. And even if you have strengthened him four or five times, you must (if he needs it) strengthen him yet again.10

As for the nature of the help to be given, one could find no more modern guideline than that suggested by Maimonides in the twelfth century:

> (The highest level of charity is) to anticipate charity by preventing poverty; namely, to assist the reduced fellowman, either by a considerable gift or a loan of money, or by teaching him a trade, or by putting him in the way of business, so that he may earn an honest livelihood; and not be forced to the dreadful alternative of holding out his hand for charity.11

This is precisely what the war against poverty is all about.

That the opportunity to earn a livelihood is a basic human right is implied in the Talmud, itself. According to Deuteronomy 4:42, a man who committed accidental homicide could take refuge in a city of asylum where "he might live." The rabbis interpreted the latter phrase to signify that such a man must be provided with the means for a livelihood and only those cities that could offer employment were selected for asylum.12 The talmudic point was that to save a man's life includes providing him with a livelihood; otherwise, he might as well be dead. Rabbi Emanuel Rackman, who has related this particular case to the philosophy of human rights, concludes:

> The right to live in a state must inevitably mean the right to work, and what was a special instance in Jewish jurisprudence must become the rule for all the inhabitants of the earth.13

Finally, the word "charity" in Hebrew is *Tzedakah,* meaning righteousness or justice. Therefore, giving to the poor should

[89]

be, for the Jew, not simply an act of love or compassion but an obligation required by law. This was a law rooted in the very nature of the universe, itself:

> Not only does man sustain man, but all nature does so. The stars and the planets, and even the angels sustain each other.14

So, interdependence is a cosmic principle that man ignores at his peril.

Discussion: What similarities can you see between the methods used by the Jewish community to help the poor and those methods used today by the government or suggested by the Freedom Budget? Compare the classical liberal's view of charity with the idea of *Tzedakah* in Jewish tradition.

Compensatory Programs in Israel

The government of Israel has for several years been following a policy of special treatment for a culturally deprived minority. Special programs have been devised for the children of "Oriental Jews" (immigrants from Arabic countries in the Middle East and North Africa) who come from homes where the level of literacy is low and where many of the simple concepts familiar to "Western" children are not taught. These "compensatory measures" tested in Israel include:

> . . . free nurseries; allocation of special funds for building equipment, and supplies; longer school day and school year programs; adaptation of the curriculum; special tutoring for teachers; counseling services; preferential acceptance to academic secondary schools 15

Through such programs more and more of these culturally disadvantaged Jews are enabled to enter the mainstream of Israeli life. The man primarily responsible for this pioneering work is Professor Moshe Smilansky, research advisor to the Israeli Minister of Education. His creative efforts have had a significant influence on Head Start and other American programs. Incidentally, Israel's experience with Oriental Jews might give pause to those who brag that "Jews made it on their own." *Any* people who, for whatever reason, have not been integrally a part of an industrial society will need tremendous help if they are to become productive members of that society.

2. Open Occupancy

"Open Occupancy" has come to mean the freedom of any individual to buy or rent a dwelling, without being excluded because of his race, color, or religion.* The Civil Rights Act of 1968 contains a fair housing provision that would by 1970, outlaw discrimination in 80 percent of the nation's homes. However, enforcement may prove to be a serious problem for many whites are still strongly opposed to having Negroes as neighbors. Among the reasons given for this opposition are: (1) "Property values will fall, and my house will be worth several thousand dollars less than it is now." (2) "Before you know it, the neighborhood will be a slum, and we will have to worry about the safety of our families." (3) "If the children play together, sure enough one out of ten will marry one." (4) "A man should have the right to dispose of his own property as he sees fit." (5) Finally, "You can't legislate morality." Let us now examine these objections.

a. Property Values

According to the Federal Housing and Home Finance Agency, the value of homes owned by Negroes rose 123 percent between 1950 and 1960. The worth of homes owned by whites rose 59 percent in the same period. In the words of Whitney Young, this means that "Negro parents are plowing in every nickel and dime they can scrape up to make life better for their children, something they couldn't always do in the past.[16] In looking more closely at these figures, the Urban League found that in Syracuse, New York, values increased by 33 percent in a neighborhood that became integrated during the decade. Similar studies made in San Francisco,

*See Opinionaire Items 14 and 20.

Portland, Baltimore, and Philadelphia, showed that the values in some integrating neighborhoods either held their own or increased as nonwhites moved in.

On the other hand, property values will surely fall in certain situations. If, when Negroes come into an area, most of the white families decide to leave, then—by the law of supply and demand—the price one could receive for his house will have to decrease. With such a large supply of homes on the market, each individual home becomes less valuable, and the seller may well suffer a financial loss. As an American Jewish Congress study explains:

> It is the mass exodus that temporarily gluts the market with offerings that depress prices—not the influx of minority groups.17

In other words, when the white families "panic and run," they, themselves, are causing the drop in prices! If they refuse to panic, then property values will follow their normal course. This kind of flight has occurred in many cities, but it does not have to happen. Studies already cited have demonstrated that in some communities the people did not run, and the standards of the neighborhood were maintained. The choice, then, must be made by each individual community.

b. Crime and Delinquency

The problem of crime in integrating neighborhoods has, according to recent studies, been exaggerated. Morton Grodzins, after surveying the data available, concludes that "lower-class Negroes . . . tend to move into lower-class neighborhoods; middle-class Negroes into middle-class neighborhoods." Since, as was seen in the previous chapter, delinquency is related not to race but to social conditions, when Negroes of one class move next door to white families of the same class, there will probably be no significant change in the neighborhood's crime rate.

But will not lower-class Negroes follow the middle-class Negroes into the neighborhood? This may happen, especially if the white families suddenly leave thereby lowering values and opening the neighborhood to the poor. However, the "piling up process" that breeds a slum does not happen until the neighborhood has become virtually all-Negro.

Of course, if any neighborhood, Negro or white, integrated or segregated, is adjacent to a slum neighborhood, some of the crime may spill over. However, criminals are easily as attracted to wealthy suburban homes as to those in integrated urban areas. In other words, so long as the conditions which breed crime exist, there is no place where one can be completely safe.

The statistics on interracial crime reported by Marvin Wolfgang are worth noting. Of the murders committed in Philadelphia from 1948 to 1952, 94 percent were *intra-racial*, that is, the victim and the offender were of the same race. Of those murders that were interracial, Negroes were victims of whites approximately three times more frequently than whites were victims of Negroes. In Menachem Amir's study of rape in Philadelphia, only 6.9 percent of the rapes were interracial: 3.6 percent involved a white offender and a Negro victim; 3.3 percent, a Negro offender and a white victim.[18] The conclusions of these as well as studies in other cities reveal that: violent crimes are in overwhelming measure most likely to be committed by a member of one race against a member of the same race; in interracial crimes, Negroes are slightly more likely to be the victims of whites than are whites to be victims of Negroes.

The point is that delinquency does not automatically increase when neighborhoods become integrated. In fact, the amount of interracial crime generally is not nearly so great as the newspaper headlines would lead one to believe.

c. Interracial Marriages

"Would you want your daughter to marry a Negro?"— eventually discussions about integration come down to the fear of interracial marriage. A Jewish parent might well respond: "I would like my daughter to marry a Jew, but for that reason I am not going to try to keep Christians (white or Negro) out of our neighborhoods or schools." However, this answer is not enough. A Jewish mother echoed a common feeling when she remarked: "If my daughter married a white Christian, I might not like the idea but I could accept it. But for her to marry a Negro—that would be too much!" Why? What is the deep-rooted objection to marriage between the races?

It is sometimes suggested that race-mixing (miscegenation) will lead to a lowering of the cultural standards developed over the centuries by the Caucasian race. After considering the slave system in the South and the concentration camps in Nazi Germany, one may find himself speaking less confidently about the cultural standards of the Caucasians. Of course, the assumption behind this fear of cultural degeneration is that the qualities of intelligence and temperament needed for the achievement of industrial progress and political democracy are racial characteristics not possessed in like measure by Negroes. That this is a fallacy has already been demonstrated in the preceding chapter.

Ashley Montagu has pointed out that prior to the Golden Age in Greece, there was a great deal of race-mixing. The *decline* of Greek culture occurred when the Greeks were generally of one racial composition. Montagu's conclusion is not, of course, that race-mixing produces a higher culture but that cultural achievement occurs when historic conditions encourage the development of that human potential which is found among all groups. To return to the UNESCO Statement on Race:

> With respect to race-mixture, the evidence points unequivocally to the fact that this has been going on from earliest times. Indeed, one of the chief processes of race formation . . . is by means of hybridization between races or ethnic groups. Furthermore, statements that human hybrids frequently show undesirable traits, physical disharmonies and mental degeneracies, are not supported by the facts. There is, therefore, no biological justification for prohibiting intermarriage between persons of different ethnic groups.[19]

i.) Problems of Social Acceptance and Marital Incompatibility

A more real difficulty with interracial marriages is that of social acceptance. Will the couple find friends? Will their children be hurt? That such problems are not insoluble is demonstrated by the fact that interracial couples do find friends, usually among liberal groups in urban or university areas. However, family experts do agree that interracial marriages are more likely than intraracial marriages to encounter difficulties, all other things being equal. Racial differences often mean that there are cultural differences which may make marital compatibility somewhat more elusive. Nevertheless, assuming that such couples may face problems that other families do not encounter, should we consider this a valid reason for keeping Negroes out of white neighborhoods and schools?

Kenneth Clark has commented, "The problem for the white liberal is to choose his own sexual partners; curtailment of this important personal freedom—as important to his own freedom as to a Negro's—cannot be determined by restrictions of the civil rights of Negroes."[20] Clark is saying that all people should have the responsibility of making their own marital choices. *Because some people may make problem producing choices is no justification for depriving millions of American Negroes of rights that white Americans demand for themselves.*

Despite all the concern, the "number of racial intermarriages in states where education is integrated" has been termed by sociologist Robert Briestelt "statistically insignificant."[21] However, as the cultural differences between the two groups decrease, the intermarriage rate could increase. Of course, if whites and Negroes do become more similar in their cultural backgrounds, the problems of social acceptance and marital incompatibility would then become less severe.

ii.) Racial Intermarriage and Jewish Tradition

While according to Jewish tradition, Jews should marry Jews, racial intermarriages are given the sanction of Jewish law, provided both partners are Jewish. In *Numbers* 12, we read that Moses married a Cushite woman, probably a Negro from Ethiopia. Aaron and Miriam criticized him for this act. Perhaps because Miriam was the chief critic, she was punished by being afflicted with leprosy, a disease believed to have been the divinely decreed punishment for the slanderer. It is interesting to note that a leper's skin becomes *white,* surely an ironic fate for one who looked down on another for being black.

Whether or not Jews will marry within their faith depends upon how deep an appreciation they have for their Jewish heritage. It is for the home and the synagogue to cultivate such appreciation. An American Jewish Congress study of this problem concluded: "An affirmative program of Jewish education, not religious ghettoizing, is the only truly effective defense against intermarriage and the best means of assuring Jewish survival."

Discussion: Segregationists may well agree that integration should be thwarted lest it lead to intermarriage and may, at the same time, contend that a white person can never be a good friend of a Negro.

There is some evidence that some Southern (and perhaps Northern) whites have a fantasy-picture of Negro men as being "oversexed."[22] Could there be any connection between this stereotype and the fear of integration and mixed marriage?*

d. The Sanctity of Property Rights

One of the most frequently stated objections to any kind of open occupancy legislation is that a man should have the right to dispose of his property as he so desires. It was noted in Chapter Three that in Jewish law (indeed, in all legal systems) the right to do what one will with his property is not considered to be absolute. Numerous limits have been placed on this right in order to safeguard other rights considered even more basic.

---

*See Opinionaire Items 3 and 19.

Therefore, the question must be asked: Why is the particular right, to sell one's property to whomever one chooses, considered so sacred as to be inviolable? It is sometimes said that if Property Right A is compromised, then Property Right B will be in danger, and soon all of man's property rights will be in jeopardy. One might reply that for centuries there have been laws restricting property rights and these laws have not led to the elimination of private property. In medieval England an innkeeper was forced by law to serve anyone who asked for service; in America, food processors are limited by health regulations as to what they can sell to the public; and private property is still very highly prized in both countries. The question is: Once the people start limiting this right, must they keep restricting until private property, itself, is eliminated, or are they able in each instance to decide when other human rights are more fundamental?

e. On Legislating Morality

It is often said that one cannot create brotherhood by passing laws, or "you can't legislate morality." The point being made is that if the people are not ready for integrated living, they cannot by laws be pushed into accepting as neighbors individuals who, for whatever reasons, they dislike. Furthermore, in a free country we should not be forced to associate with anyone we would rather avoid.*

Advocates of open occupancy legislation reply that Negroes are not asking for the friendship of their neighbors. They are quite willing to be ignored by those who do not like them. No white man would be required by such legislation to associate with all the people on his block.

Furthermore, while an open occupancy law does not attempt to "order love," it may create conditions under which reduction of prejudice is more likely. There is ample evidence that the executive order issued in 1948 by President Truman, integrating the armed forces, had the effect of decreasing some prejudices, once the men discovered through

---

*See Opinionaire Item 4.

working together that people of the other race were actually human.*

Of course, whites may experience discomfort by being forced to have Negroes on their block. To help you decide how this discomfort should affect the moral choice for or against open occupancy, compare the psychological pain of whites who find Negroes in the neighborhood with the suffering of the thousands of Negroes who, being excluded, must live in the ghetto.

Arguments in Favor of Open Occupancy

1.) *Less overcrowding in the Negro areas.* As Morton Grodzins has pointed out, open occupancy legislation cannot be expected to eliminate the dark ghettos, because many Negroes do not have either the money or desire to live in integrated areas.[23] Nevertheless, the Negro neighborhoods would be somewhat less crowded and therefore slightly more livable. There is also an important psychological difference between being locked in a ghetto from which one cannot escape and living near only members of one's race as a matter of choice.

2.) *Stabilization of property values in border neighborhoods.* As was noted, the primary reason for the decline in property values is the mass flight of whites who leave at the first sign of integration. However, if Negroes were allowed to live anywhere they could afford, they would distribute themselves more evenly throughout the white population rather than focus upon one particular border neighborhood. This would mean: (a) With Negroes more widely scattered, individual areas would be less likely to be "invaded" by a large group of Negro families; therefore, white residents would no longer feel so threatened as to flee at the first sight of a Negro neighbor; (b) There would be no place for whites to hide, since all areas would be open to Negro residents; and if there is no place to hide, one may as well stay put. Thus,

---

*See Opinionaire Item 20.

if the 1968 Civil Rights Act should be strictly enforced in both city and suburb, the urban exodus could be significantly slowed.

3.) *Open occupancy would decrease the human suffering within the Negro community.* Do you recall the chasidic story, in which one man says to another, "If you do not know what gives me pain, how can you say that you truly love me?" It is often difficult to know what gives pain to our fellowman, but we can try to identify with him.

How would you feel if you were a Negro who had to suffer the indignity of having door after door slammed in his face? There was the case of a veteran who had grown up in a Philadelphia suburb, had served in World War II and Korea, had come home as an electronics technician and had looked for a house in his old neighborhood.[24] He was told in effect: "Welcome home, O Defender of Democracy, but buy a house somewhere else!" He encountered discrimination in its clever and not so clever forms: The key is lost; the property was just taken off the market; the salesman is out. How would you feel having saved your money so you and your family could have a better life, only to be told: Go live among your own kind behind the ghetto walls? Now, multiply your feelings by thousands, for there are thousands of Negroes who do feel themselves strangled by the white noose around the dark ghetto.

There is one aspect of the Negro's pain that may be particularly hard for white people to imagine. As was stated in Chapter Three, we often claim certain rights for ourselves simply by virtue of our being human. For example, the right to live where we can afford without being penalized because of our race or religion we may consider part of our fundamental right to life, liberty, and the pursuit of happiness. Now, when we claim a *human* right for ourselves and then deny it to someone else, we are, in effect, saying to that someone else: "You are not *really* human." When we deny the Negro those rights *due to all* men, we are denying his very manhood, the essential dignity of his being. Does this help you see why he so urgently demands to live where he can afford:

[99]

not only because he wants (what we all want) the house that can best meet his needs but also because as a human being he must insist that he has just as much right to buy the house of his choice as has any other American.

4.) *Integrated neighborhoods will make for better human relations throughout American society.* Social psychologists (Brophy, Sherif, and others) have demonstrated that one of the most effective ways of reducing prejudice is by creating situations in which people of different groups but of equal status come together in pursuit of common goals. Neighbors do generally have both equal status and such common goals as working together for better schools, libraries, and recreational facilities. Therefore, in integrated neighborhoods, where residents become aware of each other and their shared interests, one can expect a reduction of prejudice. Should such integration take place throughout America, our country could move significantly closer to realizing its democratic ideals.

Integration in Jewish Tradition

On the question of integration, Jewish tradition has understandably expressed mixed feelings. Judaism is, of course, committed to the ideal of human brotherhood. However, the gentile world has often been considered such a threat to the physical and spiritual well-being of the Jewish community that integration into that world was at times discouraged. For example, in talmudic times not only could a Jew not sell cattle to a Gentile (see Chapter Two), but he was also not allowed to drink any wine or food prepared by him nor could he even accept from him a dinner invitation, even though special arrangements had been made to satisfy the requirements of the dietary laws![25]

However, when Jews began settling in very small groups throughout Europe, integration became an economic necessity. They, therefore, began trading freely with Gentiles and eating their bread, and the law was amended accordingly.

Still it remained forbidden to drink with Gentiles when the purpose was purely recreational.[26] The rabbis feared that if the Jews of these tiny communities engaged in unlimited socializing with non-Jews, the consequence would be assimilation or, at least, a weakening of loyalty to the law.

Despite their fears of the gentile world, the rabbis ruled in favor of open occupancy with one reservation: When the children of Israel would one day return to Zion, the *ger toshav* (or, resident alien) would be allowed to live in any place he might choose in all of Israel, except (*for security reasons*) in the strategic border areas or in the capital, Jerusalem. This extremely theoretical law might be taken to imply that the rabbis favored equal housing opportunity in principle, but made exceptions when they believed that non-Jews posed a dangerous threat to the very existence of the community.[27]

With the dawn of emancipation, new conditions gradually led to a further relaxation of self-segregating laws although at first the rabbis protested the behavior of the "integrating" Jews. In eighteenth-century Germany, where there were many new and widely scattered Jewish communities, Jews were staying at gentile hotels, contributing to non-Jewish charities and giving presents to gentile friends on the secular new year.[28] In twentieth-century America, of course, the trend towards increasing contacts across religious lines has continued, and few Jews today have even heard of the restrictive laws promulgated for another era.

Turning from *halachah* to agadic literature (from law to lore), we find the principle of open occupancy most forcefully set forth in the *midrash* about Adam which was quoted, in part, in the previous chapter. The rabbis dramatized the idea that our humanity is more fundamental than our racial differences by stating that Adam was created out of yellow, white, black, and red soil. The *midrash* then continued: "Therefore, the earth can declare to no race or color of man that you do not belong here; this soil is not your home!"[29] Our common humanity implies that no man should be excluded from any plot of land because of the color of his skin.

Finally, there is a fascinating chasidic dialogue that lends support to the thesis that integrated neighborhoods should make for better human relations:

> Question: It is written in Proverbs: "As in water face answereth to face, so the heart of man to man." Why does the verse read "in water" and not "in a mirror"?

> Answer: Man can see his reflection in water only when he bends close to it, and the heart of man too must lean down to the heart of his fellow; then it will see itself within his heart.30

Once a man looks into his neighbor's heart and sees himself, he will have learned that he and his neighbor share the same basic hopes and fears and dreams. Therefore, a social policy, such as integration, that makes possible genuine communication, can be an important method of teaching the brotherhood of man.

Discussion: From the above it should be clear that one can find a quote or two from Jewish tradition to support either side of the open housing controversy. The *midrash* on Adam and the chasidic comment on Proverbs lend support to open housing, while the self-segregating laws might give some rationale for resisting integration. The question, then, becomes: Which view of open housing is more consistent with the fundamental moral ideal, "Love thy neighbor as thyself"?

Among the questions one might explore to arrive at a conclusion are the following (recalling the perspective suggested in Chapter One): Would the total consequences of open occupancy lead to an increase or decrease of human suffering? Or (invoking Hillel's summary of the Torah) "What is displeasing to thee, do not do to your fellowman." Which would displease you more, being forced not to discriminate in the sale of your property or being forcibly excluded from desirable neighborhoods because of your group identity?

It is sometimes stated that predominantly Jewish neighborhoods are necessary for the development of a high quality of Jewish religious and cultural life; therefore, integration should be resisted. Is the premise (that integration will lead to a decline in Jewish life) correct? If so, should such neighborhoods be "protected" by attempting to exclude other groups? Is there something inconsistent about restricting the rights of our fellowman for the sake of Jewish life?

3. Integrating the Schools

When, in 1954, the Supreme Court ruled against compulsory segregation, the majority opinion included in its
argument the following finding from an earlier case:

> Segregation of white and colored children in public schools has
> a detrimental effect upon the colored children. The impact is
> greater when it has the sanction of the law: for the policy of
> separating the races is usually interpreted as denoting the
> inferiority of the Negro group. A sense of inferiority affects
> the motivation of a child to learn. Segregation with the
> sanction of the law, therefore, has a tendency to retard the
> educational and mental development of Negro children and
> to deprive them of some of the benefits they would receive
> in a racially integrated school system.[31]

As has already been noted, only token integration took
place in the South during the next ten years, although in
the not so Deep South there is now evidence of a significant
number of Negroes attending integrated schools: 17.2 percent in Texas and 16.3 percent in Tennessee, as of 1965-6.

Meanwhile, in the North, where school segregation was
never legalized, the proportion of predominantly Negro
schools has been *increasing* because of (1) the segregated
housing pattern and (2) a growing number of whites leaving
the city for the suburbs or sending their children to private
schools. In the larger cities, segregation is most pronounced
in the elementary schools. In Manhattan, in 1963, 77 percent of elementary school students were nonwhite. In
Philadelphia, in 1965, more than 50 percent of all public
school children were Negro. It is predicted that in Washington, D.C., by 1970, 90 percent of the student body will be
nonwhite.[32]

The Demand for Integration Now

In view of the increasing rate of *de facto* segregation of the
school population in large urban areas, some but not all civil
rights leaders are demanding immediate steps to assure true

integration. Among the steps being urged are the following:

a. *Busing.* While generally considered a temporary expedient, busing children from more crowded slum schools to less crowded middle-class schools seems reasonable to proponents of integration. Attempts are generally made to send the more motivated children to the predominantly white schools so that they will be able to hold their own. "Reverse busing"—that is, taking white children into predominantly all-Negro schools, has been so bitterly resented by white parents that it is not thought of as a practical program.

b. *Educational Parks.* At one time called "the campus plan," this proposal would establish an entire complex of educational facilities (elementary, middle, and high school) that would serve a very large area. These parks would hopefully become models of quality education, thus encouraging white families to return from the suburbs to the city. Somewhat similar is the "central school technique" by which certain schools are used to serve all children of a single grade in the city.

c. *The Princeton Plan.* Here is a method aimed at achieving a moderate increase in integration. White and Negro schools located fairly close to each other are paired, one school housing, for example, the first three grades; the other, the three upper grades.

d. *Open Enrollment.* Parents may send their children to any school in the system so long as that school has sufficient space. This plan was tried in New York City but was terminated after a few years, apparently because relatively small numbers of Negroes were willing to send their children to distant schools and because the schools to which disadvantaged children might be sent were becoming overcrowded.

e. *City-Suburban School Merger.* So long as the wealthy tend to live in the suburbs and the poor, in the city, the suburban system will have the funds to build fine schools while the city may not have the resources to maintain an adequate standard of education for all its children. Also, so long as these two systems coexist, integration on a large scale will be almost impossible, because the proportion of white children in the city is diminishing. To correct the economic inequity and to foster integration, some civil rights leaders have proposed a merger of the city and suburban school districts.

Objections to Integration Now

The main criticism of such programs is that at the present time integrated education cannot be quality education. When children from culturally deprived lower-class homes attend schools with those of middle-class backgrounds, the latter—it is claimed—will be held back in their academic achievement by the presence of youngsters who have had the misfortune of a disadvantaged background. Hence the cry: "Bring them up to our level . . . don't drag us down to theirs!"

There are, of course, other arguments: Busing or educational parks would destroy the neighborhood school that has made it possible for teachers to have better communications with the parents and for children to have school friends in the neighborhood. Also, integration may lead to interracial dating and eventually marriage. However, the main objection from the white parent is usually the fear that integration will lower his own child's academic achievement.

In the next section we shall ask whether or not this is a realistic fear. But real or imagined, the very fact that so many white parents are apprehensive over the effects of racial mixing on quality education has made large-scale integration a very distant prospect. If integration must wait, as Charles Silberman has suggested, until the schools in all slum areas "are brought up to the level of the best schools in the city," then to push vigorously the various integrationist proposals becomes a waste of energy and a disservice to Negro children.[33] How so?

Ardent integrationists may easily encourage the belief that all-Negro schools have to be inferior, and this belief helps them become inferior. Oscar Handlin has contended that this view has no factual basis: There "is no evidence that racial balance, itself, improves the capacity of the under-privileged to learn."[34] (This he wrote before the 1967 study of the U.S. Commission on Civil Rights. See below.) Among Negro leaders, Kenneth Clark and Rev. Eugene Callender have argued that the children of Harlem cannot wait for the vague promise of integration, but, having only one life to lead, require massive remedial programs now, so that there might be excellent education in all-Negro schools.[35]

The Case for Integration Now

1. Segregation and Learning

Advocates of speedy integration will find their case well argued and thoroughly documented in the report titled *Racial Isolation in the Public Schools,* published in 1967 by the United States Commission on Civil Rights. The commission found that Negro children in predominantly white schools do achieve more rapidly than Negro children in pre-dominantly Negro schools. The question is: Why?

Two important factors are social class and the quality of the education. A middle-class background, because of the educational level and values of the parents, is more con-ducive to a child's education than a lower-class background. Since most majority white schools are middle-class and most majority Negro schools lower-class, the atmosphere of the majority white school is more likely to encourage learn-ing. At the commission hearing, the mood of one lower-class predominantly Negro school was succinctly described by one of the students: "If you cooperated with the teacher and did your homework, you were a 'kook.' "[36] Those children who might under other circumstances be motivated to learn are, in many a slum school, under pressure from their peers to resist education.

As for the quality of the education, compared with children in majority white schools, students in majority

Negro schools can usually expect fewer library books, more crowded classrooms and poorer teaching. As Isaiah Robinson, chairman of a Harlem Parents Committee, stated: "Having a white child sit next to mine is no guarantee that mine will learn, but it is a guarantee that he will be taught."[37] He was making the point that the white community simply will not vote the funds needed to develop quality education in the slum schools. However, such funds are available for schools with white children. Accepting these premises, the conclusion is obvious: Negro parents should send their children to integrated schools.

The commission found that when class background and the quality of teaching were the same, racial composition of the classroom, by itself, *did* affect learning:

> Relatively disadvantaged Negro students perform better when they are in a class with a majority of similarly disadvantaged white students than when they are in a class with a majority of disadvantaged Negroes . . . Negro students in majority white schools with poorer teachers generally achieve better than similar Negro students in majority Negro schools with better teachers![38]

But why should Negro children learn more rapidly simply because the skin color of most of their classmates is white?

Negro schools are looked upon by the community at large as inferior, less desirable, and of lower status. The students naturally accept this judgment, and having a poor opinion of their schools develop a poor opinion of themselves. Such feelings of inferiority are bound to inhibit the learning process. Also, being in a segregated school not by choice but because the community will not allow integrated living—this, too, is enough to depress a young mind. After a student exchange between a white suburban school and an all-Negro high school in Cleveland, one of the Negro students clearly articulated the damaging effect of racial isolation: "Well, it was nice of them to come down to the zoo to see us."[39] Rare, indeed, is the child who can learn—if he thinks his class is a cage and his school, a menagerie.

One might argue that while integration may help Negro

children overcome some of their special handicaps, the same result can be achieved through compensatory programs in the lower-class Negro schools. However, the commission reported that Negro children attending majority white schools that had *no* compensatory programs showed greater progress than did Negro children of similar background who participated in such programs in majority Negro schools. Of course, "preferential treatment" for the disadvantaged is only just beginning and more effective techniques will surely be developed. Still, the commission's study makes clear that today integration, especially when it involves both race and class differences, can make a tremendous difference in the life of the less fortunate child: "When disadvantaged Negro students are in class with more advantaged whites, their average performance is improved by as much as two grade levels!"[40]

2. Integration and the Academic Achievement of the White Child

As we have already observed, the main stumbling block in the way of school integration is the belief of many white parents that integrated education cannot be quality education. What has the commission to say on this crucial issue? This much seems clear from the samples studied:

> The achievement of white students in classes which are roughly *half or more than half* white is no different from that of similarly situated students in all white classes.[41] (Italics author's)

That is to say, when, in integrated schools, *less than half* the children are Negroes, then the achievement of the white children in the sample tested was not significantly affected. However, as we have noted above, there is an increasing number of large cities where the Negro proportion of the school population has reached 60 percent, and is heading towards 90 percent! If there should be large-scale integration in these cities, then the student bodies of almost all of the schools would be *more than half Negro*. How would this situation affect the achievement of the white students?

An examination of the commission's statistics suggests that under present conditions the white children in such schools, *if they were in majority Negro classes,* would on the average achieve slightly less than would similar children in 90 percent white schools. It should be remembered that conditions can and do change. Ultimately the level of learning in schools, whatever their racial composition, depends upon the will of and resources available to each community.

So that integrated schools would also provide quality education, the commission has made the following recommendations:

a. Congress should establish a uniform standard providing for the elimination of racial isolation in the schools. For example, if integrated schools were considered, those that are 10 percent to 50 percent Negro, then quality education could surely be preserved.

b. The states should develop the means for meeting the standard. This would have to mean, in many metropolitan areas, a realignment of school districts, somewhat akin to the city-suburban merger described above.

c. Federal financial assistance should be made available to states and cities to provide for construction of new facilities and improvement in the quality of education in all schools.[42]

3. The Human Relations Consequences of Integration

Advocates of integration insist that the attitudes children develop in school are just as much a part of the quality of their education as is their academic achievement. In a democracy, we should be teaching children to accept one another as human beings and not to make prejudgments about others because of their race or religion, and this can best be done in an integrated school. As for the fear of interracial marriage (as was noted above), its frequency does not seem to vary significantly with the degree of school integration. In any case, choosing one's mate should be a matter of free choice, and Negroes should not be deprived of equal educational opportunity in order to shield whites from the challenge of this personal freedom. As for the "Neighborhood School," it is not, for the integrationist, such a sacred value. For years before the Supreme Court decision of 1954, large numbers of white parents have been sending their children to distant private schools. Of course, the neighborhood school has its advantages, but the public interest is better served by integrated schools that give all the children a quality education.

Jewish Tradition, Books, and Brotherhood

Judaism has exalted the values of both learning and love. "The world," states the Talmud, "rests only upon the breath of children in school."[43] Many Jewish parents leave integrating neighborhoods, because they fear for the educational development of their children. But human brotherhood is also a Jewish ideal: Recall Rabbi Heschel's statement that when we segregate our fellowman (created in God's image), we segregate God.[44] A conflict may well develop between the desire to realize both these ideals, to encourage integration and to assure oneself or one's child of the best possible education. How can such a conflict be resolved?

The Jewish philosopher, Saadia, echoing Aristotle, said that any ideal could lead to harm, if pushed to an extreme.[45] We might, therefore, be wary of so exalting learning as to feel that a high school that does not offer calculus in its curriculum is grossly inadequate. By the same token, we might take care not to allow a child's development to be stifled in a school that cannot meet his basic educational needs for the sake of a worthy but distant social goal. To all those who can afford educational advantages, our tradition would caution: Should one accept for himself (or his children) opportunities that are closed to others in his society, he places himself under a solemn obligation never to rest until all of his fellowmen have the very same chance for self-fulfillment that he enjoys.

Discussion: Critics have charged that the Civil Rights Commission's proposal that Congress decide at which point there are too few or too many Negroes in every school in America is an unwarranted extension of federal power into the domain of state and local government. What is your opinion?

Imagine you live in the suburbs and attend a predominantly white school (perhaps you do). Would you (or do you) favor the merging of your school district with that of the city, so that Negro children might have the opportunity of attending majority white schools? Under what conditions (if any) do you think most suburbanites would accept such a plan?

Is it necessary to have school integration in order to teach children to respect one another as human beings regardless of religious and racial differences? Can home, church or synagogue be trusted with the responsibility of teaching humane attitudes, or should the school share this responsibility?

Imagine that Negro children have been bused into your school from a slum neighborhood. They were well received and were seen to improve markedly in the new surroundings. But then with new white children from your own neighborhood, your classes suddenly grew in size from 30 to 36. You can still learn the required subjects, but with 36 in the class you are not learning quite so rapidly. The disadvantaged Negro children, once returned to their own neighborhood, would be attending classes of 40 to 50 children and would experience the other problems of racial isolation. The question is this: Would you favor (1) sending the Negro children back to the school in their own area; (2) continuing the policy of admitting disadvantaged Negro children so long as your school environment was superior to theirs; (3) not allowing the admission of any *additional* children from the slums?

An Emotional Block?

In this chapter we have been exploring some of the proposals that have been voiced by leaders of the "Negro Revolt." The main arguments, for and against, these policies and programs have been summarized. However, the bitter resistance to these programs in the white community has caused many blacks to feel that all attempts to become integrated into the so-called mainstream of American life are futile. Rather than be so concerned with becoming part of the system, the black American should develop his own community and culture and should demand the right to determine his own destiny. This movement toward self-determination and community control has posed a challenge to whites in general and Jews in particular. If we are to respond intelligently to the challenge, we must understand the new ideology, explore the arguments for and against local control, and face squarely the problem of Negro-Jewish tensions. These are the purposes of the following section.

SECTION TWO

Allies or Adversaries?

Chapter Six

BLACK SELF-DETERMINATION AND
JEWISH NATIONALISM

The Jewish liberal is under attack from all sides. Black militants are saying: "You're a phony. When the chips are down, you'll side with the establishment." One young black college student, after discussing the "Black Revolution" with a rabbi in his home, finally remarked that no matter what the rabbi might say, he could never trust him. Why? Because he had wall-to-wall carpeting.

White conservatives may chortle over the liberal's discomfort: "See, I told you so. Your sentimental do-goodism has brought us nothing but grief, spelled Black Power. Even Jewish intellectuals are now warning that the simplistic assumptions of liberal-integrationist strategy should be reexamined. Is it really true, they wonder, that Negro and Jewish interests are in harmony? If it is hard to be a Jew, it is becoming even harder to be a Jewish liberal. What has happened?

By 1968, the ideas and attitudes associated with the cry, "Black Power," had coalesced into a movement toward self-determination. This movement, supported by an articulate minority within the black community, espouses an ideology and strategy that leave no place for the traditional liberal-Jewish Negro alliance for civil rights. It will be the purpose of this chapter to examine this new mood and then to compare and contrast its ideas and programs with national movements in Jewish experience. Such a comparative study is presented as a means of gaining insight into the social philosophy of black self-determinism and as an introduction to more specific study of its programs and its implications for American Jews.

1. The Pursuit of Power

According to Harold Cruse, a leading ideologist of the new movement, the black man has been misled into believing that integration into white America is possible and desirable.[1] Given white racism, integration is not only impossible but is undesirable: why should the black man want to become part of a corrupt society? Therefore, Afro-Americans, instead of futilely trying to dissolve into a melting pot that rejects them, should develop their own ethnic possibilities, their own culture and, above all, their own political power. After all, the other ethnic groups have power: WASPs, Irish, Italians, Jews. In an America of cultural pluralism, why should the blacks be different?

Stokely Carmichael and Charles Hamilton have made clear the kind of power being sought:

> Black and colored people are saying in a clear voice that they intend *to determine for themselves the kinds of political, social, and economic systems they will live under.* Of necessity this means that the existing systems of the dominant, oppressive group—the entire spectrum of values, beliefs, traditions, and institutions—will have to be challenged and changed. It is not to be expected that this fundamental scrutiny will be led by those who benefit or even have expectations of benefit from the status quo.[2] (Author's italics)

The key phrase is "to determine for themselves." Self-determinists at times speak of "their share of power," but this share generally seems to mean the power *completely* to control the political, social, and economic systems under which they live. This would include control over the schools, businesses, and law enforcement agencies that affect the lives of black Americans. Such self-rule is not a sharing of power in the usual interpretation of cultural pluralism, in which each ethnic group (in theory) develops its own potential, but at the same time works out an accommodation or balance between its interests and the interests of other groups. To such a "liberal" interpretation of cultural pluralism, Eldridge Cleaver would no doubt respond that Afro-Americans form a colony in the heart of the "mother-country."[3] Under these conditions, what is needed is not accommodation but autonomy.

[116]

2. A Radical Separatism

For there to be black self-determination, the "existing systems . . . will have to be challenged and changed." How radical a change in the total society is being demanded? Harold Cruse has suggested that some black power advocates are essentially reformists, concerned only with blacks controlling and then leading reforms within their own community, sort of a black administration of "the colony."[4] Cleaver, however, has linked his call for self-determination with a revolution that would create a classless socialistic society for both blacks and whites.[5]

Some self-determinists advocate a greater degree of separatism than others. According to Robert Browne, some believe that "coexistence with white America is possible within the national framework if only the white will permit the Negro to develop as he wishes and by his own hand rather than in accordance with a white-conceived and white-administered pattern."[6] However, others hold that complete separation is the only answer: for example, the Malcolm X Society of Detroit rejects United States citizenship and claims five Southern states for the new Black Republic. Cleaver seems to combine the two approaches by urging immediate decentralization and community control within the United States and postponing the land question until Afro-Americans have enough political muscle to force the establishment to talk in terms of territory.[7] Although only a few suggest a return to Africa, Congressman Nix of Philadelphia was pursuaded to introduce a bill calling for federal subsidy for those blacks who do wish to return.

Given such a radical separatist ideology, the traditional coalition with white middle-class liberals appears out of the question. Carmichael and Hamilton have written that coalitions must be based on real interests rather than moral sentiment and have added pointedly that the secure and the insecure do *not* have the same interests: the rabbi with wall-to-wall carpeting will be on the other side of the barricade.[8] Perhaps an alliance could be developed between the blacks and the poor whites; perhaps also, Cleaver adds, with some of the younger generation that has been labeled the "New Left."[9] Meanwhile, the whites could be most valuable if they would work against racism within their own community.

3. Black Culture and Pride

The cultural dimension of black self-determination is of vital importance. Robert Browne considers the key question dividing blacks to be: "whether the American Negro is a cultural group, significantly distinct from the majority culture in ways that are ethnically rather than socioeconomically based."[10] Lerone Bennet has replied eloquently in the affirmative: "Soul" is "a metaphorical evocation of Negro being as expressed in the Negro tradition." The values of Soul include:

> A relaxed noncompetitive approach to being, a complex acceptance of the contradictions of life, a buoyant sadness, a passionate spontaneity, and a gay sorrow.[11]

The cultivation of racial pride can take the crude form that "black is right," or the higher form that nonwhite values are valid as complements to white values.

Once black Americans become part of the movement towards self-determination and feel pride in their race and culture, then they may well undergo a beneficial psychological transformation, a "creative leap into being." In less poetic language, they may develop a more wholesome respect for themselves that would enable them better to fulfill their potential. It was no coincidence that Malcolm X, just after he had in prison become a black Muslim, picked up a dictionary and memorized it![12] To Ossie Davis, who delivered his eulogy, Malcolm X symbolized to the Negro his manhood: he told the black man that the only way to self-respect was to get off his knees and fight his own battles.[13]

4. From Pride to Prejudice

The movement towards self-determination has in large measure been generated by the frustration of blacks who no longer believe in the "American dream." This frustration is sometimes expressed in the use of revolutionary tactics to compel the establishment to give in, and in highly symbolic language that can lend itself to anti-Semitic demagoguery. As was noted in Chapter Two, such emotional release that bears "little direct relation to the solution of the problems which caused the frustrations" has been labeled by Earl Raab "Black Expressivism." This is in marked contrast to "Black Positiveness," with its stress on healthy group-pride and the development of a political power base that would enable the Negro "to take a serious part in American pluralism."[14]

In terms of Raab's categories, positiveness becomes expressivism when the *sharing* of power implied by cultural pluralism becomes a demand for total self-determination, and when healthy pride in one's own group becomes transformed into bitter attacks on other groups by means of inflammatory generalizations and stereotypes. The failure of the majority of the white community to be responsive to the urgent needs of Afro-Americans has led some self-determinists to generalize about all whites and to label as enemies or conspirators all those who do not agree with their particular solution.

Chapter Eight will deal with the implications of this "expressivist" mood for the Jewish community. For the moment, it is sufficient to note that just as whites object to sweeping generalizations by black militants, so whites, themselves, should be on guard against generalizing about black self-determinists. There are significant differences among them, differences in the degree of separation advocated, in the amount of power demanded, and in the willingness to consider the needs of others.

Lerone Bennet began his book on *The Negro Mood* with a quotation from Hillel:

If I am not for myself, who will be for me? If I am for myself alone, what am I? If not now, when?[15]

The American Jew should recognize the tremendous importance of being for oneself and should also feel the anguish behind the black man's crying: If not now, when? The key question then becomes: In the coming struggle over the distribution of power, can all Americans remember Hillel's second question: If I am for myself alone, what am I?

5. A Historic Perspective

According to Bayard Rustin, separatism has been proposed and widely discussed during three different periods in American Negro history, each time as a response to the frustration of great expectations.[16] After the Civil War the hope of freedom was raised only to be dashed by the withdrawal of the Union Army from the South. Then it was that Booker T. Washington said, in effect: There is no possibility for the Negro to become truly a part of this nation; therefore, he should separate himself from such ambitions and concentrate on developing a high moral character. After World War I, hopes again rose, since a war had been fought to make the world safe for democracy. However, the twenties brought the rise of the Ku Klux Klan and a series of lynchings. The consequent despair was expressed in Marcus Garvey's campaign to buy ships and return to Africa. Finally, after World War II, the Supreme Court desegregation decision of 1954 and the Civil Rights Acts of 1964 and 1965, hopes once again were raised, and once again were crushed when it became clear that slums could not be eliminated by laws assuring theoretical equality. That is why some black Americans are saying, in effect: "If you will not let us in your world, the least you can do is let us run our own."

Discussion: Do you believe there is justice in the basic claim of the self-determinist; that since he is barred from the white man's world, he should be able to run his own? Why have other ethnic groups in America not demanded total community control? For what reasons have black Americans had more difficulty entering the mainstream of American life than have other ethnic groups?

Can you conceive of an America in which each ethnic group would have total control over its own destiny? What would be the problems of such a society?

What conclusions might one draw from Rustin's historic perspective? Does this mean that should the black American find truly equal opportunity in America, there would no longer be any reason for a separatist trend? What are the chances of such opportunity being offered?

Self-Determination in Jewish Experience

Cruse, Cleaver, and others have noted the similarities between the development of Jewish nationalism and the beginnings of black national awakening. Cruse has suggested that Jews who, themselves, have insisted on the development of their own cultural life have not been sufficiently sensitive to the needs of blacks to develop *their* ethnic potential.[17] Cleaver has urged blacks to learn from Theodor Herzl and set up a "government in exile."[18] On the other hand, some Jewish leaders have stressed the profound differences between Jewish nationalism and black self-determination. By observing some fascinating similarities and some significant differences the reader might better understand the challenge posed by this articulate minority of Afro-Americans.

1. Response to Shattered Dreams

The movement towards Jewish self-determination, like black separatism in American History, also followed the shattering of the dream of integration. In Russia, under the relatively benign reign of Alexander II (1861-81), the Jewish community was encouraged to believe that the night of feudal oppression was ending, as the Czar lifted anti-Semitic restrictions and allowed Jews to work in textile shops, tanneries, and tobacco factories. Some Jews were even able to become *maskilim,* enlightened intellectuals, wise in the cosmopolitan ways of Western Europe. However, the "revolution from above" came to an abrupt halt when the Czar decided that he had made enough concessions to the masses, whereupon he was promptly assassinated by a revolutionary group of peasants. His successor, Alexander III (1881-94), gave a free hand to anti-Semites who lost no time murdering Jews in Odessa, Kiev, and other cities. The new Czar instituted the May Laws which prohibited Jews from moving into any village and allowed villagers to expel undesirable inhabitants; thus Russian Jewry was forced to live, crowded and impoverished in cities and towns, from Minsk to Odessa. Under Nicholas II, the oppression became even more vicious, climaxed by pogroms in the Ukraine which, in 1904, spread northward to Minsk, Lodz, and Brest-Litovsk.

Out of the disillusion of dashed hopes, there arose Leo Pinsker, son of a cosmopolitan *maskil,*who, after the pogroms of 1881, gave up the dream of integration and became the first Jew to advocate nationalism as an answer to anti-Semitism. The solution Pinsker advocated in his pamphlet, *Autoemancipation,* was not Palestine (insufficient industrial potential!) but a territory elsewhere, perhaps in North America—shades of the Malcolm X Society.[19]

There were other Russian Jews who had a different dream that was also dashed. They were the intellectuals and workers who had joined the Russian Social Democratic party which was dedicated to a working class revolution aimed at the overthrow of the Czarist regime. Some Jewish radicals saw no purpose at all in retaining their cultural heritage and became assimilated into the universal struggle to achieve a classless society. (They might be compared to most of the Negroes in the American Communist party in the 1930's who saw nothing positive in their black heritage to perpetuate.)

However, these revolutionary Jews were in for a shock. When "the workers of the world" finally united, they united against the Jews in the pogroms of 1881 and 1904. How then could Jewish socialists merge with the RSDP? There were specific Jewish interests to consider. In the words of Arkady Kremer, founder of the Yiddish-oriented anti-Zionist Bund:

> A general union of all Jewish Socialist organizations will have as its goal not only the struggle for general Russian political demands; it will have the special task of defending the specific interests of the Jewish workers.[20]

There were other reasons for the formation of various cultural or national movements among the Jewish workers, but the Bund and, even more so, Ber Borochov's Poale Zion (Labor Zionists) in the Ukraine were born out of a loss of faith in the Russian proletariat.

In Western Europe, too, the dawn of new hope was followed by disillusion, at least in the mind of Theodor Herzl, an assimilated Viennese journalist. For the Jews in the West, including Herzl, the French Revolution was a kind of emancipation proclamation which freed them for integration into the life of Europe. Then came the trial of Captain Dreyfus which unleashed a tidal wave of anti-Semitism that was part of a Church-Army-Royalist attack against the Republic of France. Most thought the trial was but the last bigoted gasp of a dying order, but Theodor Herzl believed that the anti-Semitism of the anti-Dreyfusards signalled the beginning of the night. For Herzl, like Pinsker, Jewish nationalism was the answer to anti-Semitism. Unlike Pinsker, Herzl became a "political activist" and devoted his life to making the dream of a Jewish state come true. So, both Jewish and Negro movements towards separatism and self-determination arose out of the disillusion of shattered dreams.

Discussion: The question remains: Granted that Herzl and Pinsker were correct in their pessimism as to the possibility for the integration of Jews into the life of Europe, are the black self-determinists equally correct in their pessimism regarding the integration of blacks into the mainstream of American society?

2. Separatist Solutions

Differences in the degree of separatism advocated by black self-determinists have previously been noted, from coexistence within the national framework to a separate state to a back-to-Africa movement. Rather amazing parallels can be found among Russian Jews at the turn of the century.

The return to Zion does remind one of the back-to-Africa movement, but with a crucial difference. There is no homeland in Africa that has an attraction for blacks comparable to that of Israel for the Jewish people. A much closer parallel to the mainstream of black nationalism were the programs of Chaim Zhitlowsky and Simon Dubnow, both of whom had great influence on the Bund.

Zhitlowsky was a leader of the Seymists, who hoped to achieve socialism in Russia through national minorities. They reasoned that integration was a fantasy of the enlightenment; the only solution was that the various cultural minorities should form their own organic communities, which they would control. A Jewish *seym* (parliament) would be run by workers and progressive members of the middle class. Eventually, the Jews should have their own territory, perhaps within Russia, itself; meanwhile a large measure of self-determination could be achieved through the Jewish national organism in exile. (This solution is astoundingly close to that advocated by Cleaver in his essay on "The Land Question and Black Liberation.")[21] Simon Dubnow propounded a program of national autonomy: the Jews should have control over their own community and should exercise that control within Russia, itself. Furthermore, in the Russian parliament, all national minorities, including the Jews, should be properly represented.[22]

Within the Bund, "autonomist" sentiments were vigorously expressed by Vladimir Medem, baptized child of assimilated parents who was moved by Czarist repression to embrace Marx and return to the Jewish people. In 1903,

[123]

when he was but 24, this young Jewish militant arose
at the convention of the RSDP in London and demanded
a separate Jewish socialist party within Lenin's revolutionary movement. When the demand was rejected, the Bund
became completely independent and called on the Russian
government to allow Jewish "community control": specifically, that the state should recognize Yiddish as a "legal
language of the realm" and should provide funds for a Yiddish
school system![2] [3]

The analogy hardly requires elaboration. The Black
Panthers have become a separate revolutionary political
party for blacks, independent of the whites on the New
Left. Some blacks would be content with the kind of
program demanded by the Bundists and Dubnow which
would include, for example, control of their own school
system. Others, like the Seymists, would look forward to
one day having a territory of their own.

The significance of this analogy is that most black
self-determinists are aiming towards an autonomist solution
(with or without territory) on American soil, rather than
towards the achievement of the Zionist-type dream of
migration to a distant land. The Jewish autonomists in
Russia failed. Russian Jewry was, in 1926, given its own
province in Birobijan, just north of Manchuria. However,
few Jews were willing to migrate to such a freezing forbidding land to become lumbermen, miners, and farmers,
and the project was abandoned.

Discussion: Are black self-determinists more (or less) likely to succeed
in gaining complete control over their own communities within
America than were the Jews within Russia?

3. Comes the Revolution

While Theodor Herzl envisioned a Jewish state that would
be a model of a liberal capitalist society, in Russia both
the Bundists and Labor Zionists were concerned with the
restructuring of the entire social system. The Bundists,
while remaining apart from Russian radicals, were working towards the revolutionary goal of the overthrow of
the Czarist regime and the establishment of the dictator-
ship of the proletariat. Ber Borochov and his Labor Zionists believed that the only way Jews could ever really be
effective as social revolutionaries would be on their own

soil. To the Bundist objection that Zionism would be just another reactionary nationalism, Borochov replied that Labor Zionism would be led by the workers, not the middle class.[24] Dubnow was concerned not with social revolution but with making sure that Jews controlled their own communities, whatever political form would be dominant.

As has been noted, most black self-determinists speak of the need for fundamental changes in the social system. Some specify a socialist goal not so very different from that dreamed of by the Bundists at the turn of the century. Others seem content to put more stress on the principle of self-determination rather than on revolutionary change either in the black community or the world-at-large.

Discussion: The analogy above raises a crucial question: The Czarist regime, as one of the last remnants of the feudal order, was ready to collapse. Is the American mixed economy that combines predominantly private ownership with a significant public sector similarly ripe for falling or is it a viable system that can meet the needs of all its citizens? In other words, is revolution really necessary?

4. Jewish Pride and Culture

Just as many a black American has found a new sense of self-respect through his identification with the movement towards national self-determination, so countless Jews found a new sense of personal dignity through Jewish nationalism. It was Leo Pinsker who wrote addressing "the establishment" of 1882:

> At present we live under the oppression of the evils you have inflicted upon us. What we lack is not genius but self-respect and the consciousness of human dignity of which you have robbed us.

The Jew, continued Pinsker, could gain self-respect through "national self-determination" that would make possible the "free, active development of our national force (and) . . . our native genius."[25] It is a fascinating coincidence that Pinsker's *Autoemancipation* began with the very same words of Hillel chosen by Bennet for the introduction to *The Negro Mood:* "If I am not for myself, who will be for me? . . ."

[125]

Without meaning to equate the personalities of Israelis and black self-determinists, there are two qualities they seem to share: an impatience with maintaining the kind of image that might win popular approval and, at times, an almost cocky self-confidence. Ossie Davis has recognized that the appeal of Malcolm X for many Negroes was just this: that he had ripped off once and for all the phony servant's smile and was willing to challenge racism wherever he found it. Could it be that part of the appeal of Israeli self-assurance to the American Jew is the willingness to disregard popular opinion when Israel's survival is at stake.

Another interesting similarity is that just as black self-determinists are convinced that the soul of the black man has a unique contribution to make to white society, so those Zionists who stressed national *culture* have made the same point about the Jewish spirit. For Ahad Ha-Am, Herzl's purely political solution of the Jewish problem was not enough. The Jewish people should prepare themselves spiritually so that their state could be truly expressive of the Jewish moral genius. Zion would then be the cultural soil from which the flower of the Jewish spirit would grow. Also A.D. Gordon, a romantic socialist Zionist in love with the soil, wrote of "the ethnic self, a peculiar pattern of mental and physical forces," that would be realized by the Jews once they were settled in Palestine.[26] Lerone Bennet, who could be considered sort of a Negro Ahad Ha-Am, has already been quoted as expressing the view that black culture has a moral contribution to make to the American scene. After denying that Negroes are any better (or worse) than whites, Bennet specified the nature of that contribution:

> . . . By the grace of God, and the whip of history, Negroes in the main have not completely assimilated those values that are driving Western man to social and spiritual suicide: acquisitiveness, for example, numbness of heart and machine idolatry. To the extent that these things are foreign to the Negro's *experience*, to that extent the Negro is uniquely qualified to take the lead in recasting the human values of our civilization.[27]

Discussion: Do you agree with Bennet that Negroes, in general, are less materialistic than whites? Does his statement remind you of any claims made by rabbis about the values of Jewish culture that have been emphasized because of the minority status of the Jewish community? Jewish cultural values have been bound up with the religion of Judaism which helped give authority to and transmit them. Can the cultural values of Afro-Americans be preserved and transmitted without a uniquely black religion?

Could the effort to develop group pride lead to an exaggeration of certain qualities of one's heritage—among blacks? among Jews? It has been said that the man who truly respects himself will not need to strike out with hostility against the world. Is this correct? If so, what might this imply about bigots among blacks or whites?

The similarities between black and Jewish self-determination have been systematically spelled out above; the differences have been alluded to or implied. Since the differences may be more important than the similarities in helping one understand the future of black nationalism in America, the following summary is offered.

Religion and Culture

There is the distinction, just noted above, between a Jewish culture historically bound to a religion continuously transmitted through the centuries and a black culture that is a secular blending of American Negro experience and almost forgotten African memories. It is worth noting that the major attempt to blend religion and black nationalism—that is, the Muslim movement—has not attracted widespread support among Negroes. Because of the religious institutions in the Jewish community, it has been possible to preserve and transmit the knowledge of its heritage through synagogues and their schools. Therefore, Jews have not needed to press the public schools to teach about Jewish heroes or about the contributions of Jewish culture through medieval and modern times. The point is that the blacks do face greater difficulties than do the Jews in transmitting a culture within American life. This might become particularly evident as the blacks make their way economically into the American mainstream. Then they, like many young Jews, could be asking: Why bother preserving our heritage in a free society? However, they, unlike the Jewish community, would not be able to fall back on a historic religion.

Land

The Jewish people had for centuries been praying for a return to one specific land where they had been the majority of the population for 1400 years and where in every century since the crushing of the community by Hadrian some Jews had dwelt. There is no land that has held a similar place in the hearts of Afro-Americans. There is also no option for black Americans comparable to the choice of America for Russian Jewry: Before 1914, the United States needed and, therefore, welcomed the oppressed and the poor of Europe to provide the labor force and become the middlemen for a rapidly expanding society. Today there is no such land that offers to blacks the opportunity of a fast growing industrial economy.

Since Afro-Americans can look neither to their own Zion nor to some other "promised land" on distant shores, their fate will probably be decided within America, itself. Indeed, Carmichael has claimed that blacks should not have to pay for land in this country:

> . . . We already own it; we paid for it with four hundred years of our sweat, our blood, and our suffering.[28]

That black America could establish an autonomous self-controlling society *à la* Dubnow or Zhitlowsky seems impossible to most white Americans. Yet, some black nationalists have reminded us that boundaries are never settled forever. The feasibility of total black self-determination within America is related to another difference between Negro and Jewish experience.

Resistance of Capitalism to Autonomous Minorities

As Ellis Rivkin has made clear in "The Age of Permanent Revolution," the "developing capitalism" of the American economy requires for its optimum functioning a single system in which there is strong central authority.[29] Furthermore, given the interdependence of the parts of an industrial state, no ethnic minority can possibly exercise *complete* control over the lives of its members. For example, full employment of blacks (and whites) depends not on who owns the stores in the ghetto but on the economic policy of the nation-as-a-whole. The quality of education for black (and white) children ultimately depends not on local control of schools (whatever its advantages) but on the resources made available by the representatives of *all* the people.

In less developed noncapitalist societies, it was more likely that cultural minorities would be given political status and even territorial rights. The Jews of Russia could conceivably have been granted a degree of autonomy; however, black Americans cannot expect an advanced industrial state voluntarily to offer self-rule to one ethnic group. It is perhaps recognition of this difficulty that has led Cleaver to speak of guerilla warfare as the means by which autonomy will be achieved.[30] It should be clearly understood that most self-determinists do *not* favor such warfare and look upon the brandishing of arms as providing the state with an excuse for brutal repressive action.

There is an alternative to the call for total autonomy in all matters affecting black people: it should be possible for the black community to attain a greater *degree* of political and economic power within American society and, therefore, a much more significant voice in national policies affecting its members. However, this is crucially different from the frequently stated goal of complete control over "the kinds of political, social, and economic systems (blacks) will live under."

Hope in America?

Jewish nationalism saw no hope for the successful integration of Jews in the life of Western or Eastern Europe. The holocaust in the West and Czarist oppression followed by a repressive Communist regime in the East confirmed their fears. *Is America different?* Does this country leave the Negro with any alternative other than a desperate struggle for separation and self-determination? To many black militants together with white members of the New Left, the answer is clearly: Of course, not. The Establishment has the power to launch a truly massive war against poverty and racism but refuses to do so. The will of the people can never force the power structure to act, because their will is, through the communications media, determined by the power structure. Therefore, the power structure must be overthrown or, at least, forced to grant blacks control over their own destinies by whatever means necessary.

The much maligned liberal persists in believing that since America does have such tremendous productive power its leaders can eventually be persuaded to devote a sufficient portion of that power to an effective effort to bring the black and white poor into the mainstream of American life. Such action would be in the national interest as it would bring an end to the present social disruption and it would also be the just thing to do. The liberal adds that demands for *total* community control, the frequent use of civil disobedience, and the threat of guerilla warfare will simply give the powers on the far right the pretext for severe repression.

This may well be the crux of the debate: Is America different? Can the black man find hope in these United States, or is there *en bererah* (no alternative) to the desperation of the embittered Afro-Americans who are declaring their own independence? The answer lies neither in debate nor in social theory. It lies in the capacity of white America to act in a manner consistent with self-interest and simple justice. It may also lie in the capacity of black militants, despite their rhetoric, to be satisfied with something less than total self-determination in a pluralistic society where no ethnic group *completely controls* the lives of its members.

That the black community would relinquish the more extreme forms of separatism in an America of true opportunity was implied by Bayard Rustin when he wrote that "class ultimately is a more driving force than color."[31] If separatism, then, is a response to the rejection of a white society that has slammed the door in the face of Negro aspiration for three hundred years, then the response to black separatism would seem to be: to open the door and make it possible for those who have been cast out to enter.

Chapter Seven

COMMUNITY CONTROL AND THE RIGHT TO POWER

"Community control of the schools is the last hope of transforming ghetto education. It offers black parents the same rights suburban parents enjoy—an elected school board accountable to them."[1] So wrote Whitney Young, director of the highly respected Urban League. Thus the movement for community control of schools has gained the support of many blacks (and some whites) who would not favor the total program of self-determination advocated by Carmichael or Cleaver. Decentralized experiments are presently being tried in several major cities, including, New York, Boston, and Washington, D. C.

Also in Washington, some black leaders are demanding that the power to appoint precinct captains and police officers be vested in local councils. Now that rehabilitation of areas gutted in the disorders of 1968 is taking place, these same leaders are claiming that the power to determine which businesses and which business owners be permitted in the black community be determined by the residents, themselves.

The numerous sit-ins on college campuses from San Francisco State to Brandeis are still further expressions of the drive for local control. Generally included in the demands is the right of black students to have their own school or department of Afro-American studies and to determine their own curriculum and admission policy. The Civil Rights movement came full circle in March, 1969, when the Department of Health, Education, and Welfare ordered Antioch College to desegregate its black studies department or face the loss of federal aid.

Of these specific issues, none has affected the Jewish community more than the controversy over decentralization and community control of schools. This chapter will, therefore, focus on this sensitive conflict-area. The issue will be defined, the pros and cons presented, and then Jewish tradition will be consulted for possible guidelines to a difficult moral dilemma. Finally the insights gained through discussion of the school issue will hopefully enable the reader better to evaluate the other proposed programs for local control.

1. What Mean These Words?

The terms decentralization and community control are ambiguous because there are so many possible variations on the same theme, ranging from purely administrative decentralization which draws relatively few objections to total control which inevitably becomes an explosive issue. Administrative decentralization has been defined as:

> . . . An approach to school organization and management that places emphasis upon making decisions closer to the scene of interaction between students and educators. It is brought about by delegating certain decision-making powers to various field administrators *within a policy framework set by the central board* that is charged under law with overall educational responsibilities for the jurisdiction it serves. (Emphasis added)[2]

The point is that while the district superintendent is given greater freedom and responsibility (e.g., to select personnel or allocate funds) the ultimate power remains in the central board.

Community participation includes:

> A variety of steps that result in a continuing working contact between those who operate the schools . . . and those who use its services and facilities (either as students, parents, or members of the general community . . .)[3]

One form of such participation is community control. This suggests that local residents take initiative and hold responsibility in the policy-making and administration of the schools of their area. There are, of course, degrees of control, ranging from the right to allocate funds to the right to select and/or dismiss personnel to the right to establish curriculum policy.

2. Arguments for Local Control

Advocates argue, as did Whitney Young, that it is a matter of simple justice for blacks to determine the policies and programs of their schools just as whites control the education of their own children. For years the black community pressed for integration, but the white world refused to open its doors. The least the whites can do, having locked the blacks out, is to let them run their own house. Even if errors are made, black parents (like whites) are entitled to make their own mistakes. As Paul Goodman has written, militants have "a right to be parochial."[4]

Community control will have beneficial effect on the motivation and, therefore, the education of the children. Once parents have responsibility for what happens in their schools, they will become much more interested in all aspects of education and this interest is bound to be transmitted to their children. As one teacher commented about the students in a community control experiment in Washington: "Kids are really beginning to sense that this is their own school."[5] Once young people feel that they or their parents can really influence their education, they will have a greater sense of worth and will be more willing to be educated.*

Because the professional staff would be accountable to members of the local community, the schools would become more responsive to the needs of that community. Those needs would be primarily quality education. That is, once parents gain significant power ". . . (they) are more

---

* In support of this view the "Coleman Report" on *Equality of Educational Opportunity*, U.S. Department of Health, Education and Welfare, 1966, is often quoted: "A pupil attitude factor, which appears to have a stronger relationship to achievement than do all the 'school' factors together is the extent to which the individual feels that he has some control over his own destiny." However, on the same page, the Coleman Report states: "Those Negroes in schools with a higher proportion of whites have a greater sense of control." Harvard educator, David K. Cohen, concludes that, according to the research available, community control cannot be expected significantly to reduce racial disparities in achievement. However, Dr. Cohen does advocate a change in the locus of authority so there may be a "more viable contract between blacks and the institutions in their neighborhoods." *Commentary* vol. 48:1, July, 1969, pp. 23-32.

likely to pay close attention to the stated mission and actual performance of the institution. . . . Responsibility comes with the power of an effective voice. In the train of responsibility, judgement, stability, and dedication to constructive purposes are likely to follow."[6]

Under a giant centralized system, innovation and imagination are rare. A teacher in the demonstration district in Ocean Hill-Brownsville commented: "It's the first time in my eight years as a teacher that I have been allowed to use unconventional methods."[7] Critics would reply that innovation and imagination can be encouraged without community control by any creative principal, and by giving local administrators more authority (administrative decentralization).

Community control is needed to combat the discrimination built into large educational bureaucracies. For example, in New York City, many Negro applicants were reportedly ruled out on the basis of oral examinations because of "Southernisms" in their speech. The written tests stressed academic competence, while the capacity to be sensitive to the needs of children was not taken into account.[8] To break into such a system, the power that comes with local control is needed. The response to this argument is that in other cities blacks have fully entered the system without such control. It is sometimes added that yesterday's discrimination does not justify discrimination against *competent* white educators who would be bypassed as a result of the sudden rise of black teachers and administrators.

It is finally claimed that when neighborhood districts compete with one another, more creative energy will be released in each community. The Bundy Report, of November, 1967, capsulized all the advantages when it made the point that the system would be opened up so "all concerned can have more authority and a greater chance to work for better education."

3. Arguments against Local Control

Critics deny that community control, in itself, can lead to greater motivation on the part of children. The real problems of urban education are so deep-rooted that no significant change will take place without the massive expenditure of funds that would offer simultaneously smaller classes, remedial programs, pre-school training, as well as greater employment opportunity for fathers and better housing. Rather than face these hard facts, some leaders of the white power structure find it much more convenient (and cheaper) to favor community control. In the absence of abundant new resources, this amounts to turning the slums over to the blacks and can only lead ultimately to even greater frustration. In a word, local control has become a panacea.

Others admit that parental participation does aid in the educational process but insist that such participation could be achieved by encouraging parents to form advisory councils that would function as a kind of cabinet to the administrator. The counter-argument is that parents will not remain involved for long unless they can have some of the power.

Still another major criticism is that such localism amounts to a regression to a segregated society and this is bad for the children. In uniracial schools, black children have a lower sense of worth than do children from similar background in integrated schools, and consequently their achievement lags behind what it would be in an integrated setting.[9] Community control, especially if it should lead to almost all black educators in black communities, would create an apartheid America. Advocates respond that there is a crucial difference between the attitudes of children whose segregation is enforced and the attitudes of those whose separatism is voluntary. Furthermore, since the white society is not about to integrate, Afro-Americans have no choice but to do their best within their own community.

The most bitter criticism revolves around the prediction that "irresponsible militants" will take over community boards. Members of home and school associations may be fearful that new aggressive leaders will emerge as spokesmen for the community that the home and school people have for years been representing. Even more fearful of a "militant takeover" are many white teachers and principals. When they speak of militants, they mean those self-determinists who believe, as do Carmichael and Hamilton, that "the principals and as many teachers as possible of the ghetto schools should be black."[10] With such parents in power, the jobs of even the finest white educators would be in jeopardy, and urban schools would lose the talents of many white educators who would prefer to pursue their careers elsewhere.

The Ocean Hill-Brownsville demonstration district is usually held up as a case in point. There a governing board was chosen in an election in which only one-fourth of the parents voted. The board appointed as one of the principals in the district a Mr. Fuentes who was quoted as saying that Negro children should be taught by Negroes and Jewish children should be taught by Jews and that only teachers of the same ethnic background can teach in ghetto schools.[11] To show its power, wrote Martin Mayer, the board either transferred or dismissed (a debatable point) one principal, five assistant principals, and thirteen teachers.[12] While the United Federation of Teachers claimed that the educators *were* dismissed, the federation added that even if this were a case of involuntary transfers, the board should have gone through established procedures including the bringing of charges and the right of appeal to the courts. After all, careers and reputations were at stake, and the district administrator, Rhody McCoy, had been quoted as saying: "Not one of these teachers will be allowed to teach anywhere in this city." Why were the teachers removed? The local board claimed they were hostile to the legitimate aspirations of Negro parents while the union claimed, quoting at least one principal, that the overwhelming majority were quite competent. In August, 1968, the ten teachers who challenged their transfers in court were all vindicated by the judge. Whatever the merits and demerits of the opposing sides, the board action and the resulting strike set off an explosion of mutual recrimination between the predominantly Jewish union and the local community, the tragic overtones of which have been felt in the Negro and Jewish communities throughout the nation.

One response to these fears is that we must at some point begin trusting one another. The basis for this trust is that black parents, like white parents, are more interested in quality education than in weilding power. This appeal is considered naive by those administrators and teachers who have had the experience of dealing with determined militants who scarcely conceal their hostility towards whites in general and often towards Jews in particular. How, they say, can one trust a revolutionary movement when its own leaders justify the taking over of a community by a small group. As John F. Hatchett has written:

> It is the quality of involvement and commitment that is crucial, and not the quantity. . . . No revolutions are won by majorities. It is the dedicated devoted few who lead and fight and prevail.[13]

So, until experience proves otherwise, apprehension will remain.

Another response to those concerned with the interests of white educators is to state frankly that some blacks *do* want to take over the better teaching and administrative jobs in their own community: why shouldn't they, after having been used as America's doormat for over three hundred years? So long as white administrators administer schools in white neighborhoods, should not blacks run the schools in their own communities?

The most ominous criticism of community control is the charge that the power structure is more than willing to allow the lower class to rise at the expense of the lower middle class. In the words of Maurice Goldbloom:

> There is a widespread movement now afoot to ally the bottom and top layers of American society against those in the middle—and especially against the organized workers. This strategy has its implicit assumptions; it stems from the belief on the one side that the first enemy of the man at the bottom is the man one step up, and on the other that the discontents of the most wretched can effectively be appeased without any expense to those at the top.[14]

Discussion: Examine each argument, pro and con, and ask yourself the questions: Do you believe that community control: (1) will aid in the education of children; (2) will make it possible for the school to become more responsive to the needs of the community; (3) will release more creative energy for educational experimentation; (4) is just, because it gives power to the powerless, or gives blacks the same kind of power that whites have?
Do you think some leaders of the white power structure might view community control as an easy way out: giving blacks the slums to run rather than really attacking poverty? . . . Do you believe that parent participation can be sustained without giving

parents a considerable share of power? Does it bother you that community control may be moving back towards a "separate but unequal" society?

What do you think of the argument that once ghetto schools are improved through community control, then integration can take place more rapidly than ever before? Are you concerned lest ardent self-determinists make it difficult if not impossible for white educators to be appointed to the more desirable positions in the inner city? Given the low status of the black community generally in America, do blacks deserve preferential treatment even if this means bypassing competent whites? Would you favor giving preferential treatment to blacks applying for new positions while simultaneously protecting white educators already in black communities from arbitrary transfer or dismissal?

4. The Will of the People

If there is one crucial issue that underlies all the arguments and counter-arguments over community control, it may be the claim that black people should be able to determine the kind of school they want for their children by selecting their own representatives to a local board. Even if so-called militants should, through the apathy of the majority, "takeover," that is no reason to withhold from the people the opportunity to choose their own leaders. The democratic process has always run the risk of poor selections made by ignorant or indifferent people. Nevertheless, it is still the best process we have. One must have faith that eventually the people after having learned from their mistakes will make those choices that are rational and wise. Is this not what America is all about?

This argument does not answer the question: how large (or small) should be the population that is polled. Members of small homogeneous communities may be more likely to know what can best meet their needs. However, being naturally concerned with their own interests, they may ignore the interests of others. Perhaps if a larger community containing more groups were the political unit, a balance of interest would make for greater fairness to all concerned. To which the black self-determinist would reply: What fairness? In America today, we will be treated fairly only when we can control our own future.

Discussion: Is it possible that a system of checks and balances might be employed to establish a genuine sharing of power in which the needs of the local community are recognized and the rights of other members of society respected?

On the issue of community control of schools would you give to a central board or to a local board the following powers: the right to allocate funds . . . to set curriculum policy . . . to appoint a district superintendent . . . to appoint principals . . . to appoint teachers . . . to discharge principals . . . to discharge teachers? What safeguards should be established so that competent teachers would not be arbitrarily dismissed?

5. Other Forms of Community Control

"A Stanford for Black People"

That blacks should have complete control over their own higher education is a fundamental part of the program of consistent self-determinists. Cleaver has explained the reason:

> We need a Stanford for black people because black people cannot relate to education that teaches them that they are inferior, and that the white people are superior, and that it's going to be that way forever because that's the way that God made it. We say let white people have their educational institutions . . . and we will be more than glad to participate in that, ten lectures or twenty lectures, or just one on the run, or none, whatever we can do to help that.[15]

> And we would want to recognize that we need institutions that can give us the education that's necessary to cope with our environment . . . with white supremacy, white racism, and with the murderous institutions of this society. We would want you to endorse that, to help us do that, to participate in that. And to give whatever you can, if it means to give instruction, if it means to build the buildings.[16]

Cleaver does envision eventually "a university of the world that can teach the whole world—all the people of the world—the true history of the world; not a racist history, not a nationalist history, but a history that can enable people to live."[17] This could be established by revolutionary blacks and whites coming together, but for the present, black institutions for blacks are required.

[139]

Some have suggested that behind the movement for separate departments of Afro-American studies is the cultural disadvantage suffered by black college students as compared with their white classmates. Because of their inferior high school education, they simply cannot compete with the white students on equal terms in the academic world, and so for their own self-esteem they need their own school with its own standards. Others have warned that the government or private foundations would be ill-advised to underwrite a course of study that might teach students to cope with "the murderous institutions of this society" by means of guerilla warfare, if necessary. Still others wonder if a university can or should sponsor a school or department over which it has no authority to protect the values of scholarship and academic freedom. Finally, there is the view of the Department of Health, Education and Welfare that separatism in any form of education is a step backward.

Discussion: Do you believe that blacks have a right to their own schools of higher education? Do you agree with the argument: Since white America has forced black children to receive inferior education, white America should be responsible for providing a college education that would build upon what young black people do bring to the university? Is black higher education the responsibility of individual universities, of the federal government, of the black community? Are there any limits that should be placed on what is taught in schools of black studies? Should black students, whose achievement has been slowed because of poor educational background, be given preference for college admission over white students who because of greater educational advantages have reached higher achievement levels?

Two other forms of community control involve the power to determine which businesses shall be in the black ghetto and the power to appoint law enforcement officials who function in the black community. In considering the pros and cons of these demands, the following questions may be helpful:

Should the Jewish community facilitate, through loan funds the establishment of black-owned businesses in black neighborhoods? Should the Jewish community urge Jewish merchants to leave slum areas? Should their leaving be facilitated by loan funds set up by Jewish community federations? Is a merchant who feels forced to charge high prices and high

interest rates because of the high cost of operating a store in a
slum neighborhood justified in doing so? How would you
answer his statement that if I were not doing this someone
else would be? What do you know about "cooperative"
businesses in which a pooling of community resources might
hold down prices?

Do you think that if the black community had the power
to appoint its own law enforcement officials, there would
be a change in its attitude towards the police? Would black-
appointed police officials be more, less, or as effective as
white-appointed in controlling crime? Would the charges of
police brutality diminish? If so, would this mean a diminished
chance for riots? How do you think white police would
feel if the control of law enforcement in the ghetto were
turned over to representatives of the people living there? Is
the demand for local control of law enforcement officers
just?

6. The Issue of Ends and Means

Behind much of the debate over community control there
is the dilemma of ends and means. One may argue: the
blacks have been deprived of power so long that for
them to achieve their fair share some people are simply
going to be hurt. This is unfortunate, but the end of
true equality for millions of disadvantaged Americans justi-
fies means that might be damaging to a relatively small
and comparatively secure group. That small group could
be competent teachers who do not get promotions or
white students who are passed over so that less academically advanced blacks might attend college. The moral
issue becomes: when, if ever, do the ends justify the means?

In Jewish tradition there is, as one might expect,
more than one answer:

> They asked the "holy Yehudi":"Why is it written: 'Justice,
> justice, shalt thou pursue.' Why is the word 'justice' repeated?"
> He answered: "We ought to pursue justice with justice, and
> not with unrighteousness."

On the other hand, Jewish law is full of instances in which
a lesser principle is violated for the sake of a higher one. For
example, one is permitted to take human life in a war of
self-defense and to tell a lie in certain instances to avoid
shaming one's neighbor.

[141]

Among the questions one might consider in determining whether some harm should be done for the sake of a worthy goal are the following: 1) Is the goal truly worthwhile? That is, how much good will actually be accomplished? 2) Are there other ways of achieving the goal, ways that would not cause the harm done by the means being proposed? 3) How great would the harm really be, should the means under consideration be used? 4) *If* there is no other way of achieving a truly desirable end, would greater harm be done by achieving it through the questionable means or by relinquishing the goal altogether?

Discussion: A. Ask these questions regarding the following situations?
(1) moving towards all black administrators in ghetto schools
(2) giving preference to black teachers in ghetto schools
(3) bypassing white students who are better qualified academically so that more blacks can receive a higher education
(4) replacing white precinct officers with black officers in the black ghetto
(5) not allowing white merchants to buy stores in an all-black neighborhood.
      B. Are there any means that should never be used no matter how compelling the ends?

In the preceding discussion of community control the charge of black anti-Semitism was mentioned in passing. The impression that this form of bigotry is rampant among blacks in general and self-determinists in particular has given many Jews a rationale for indifference or hostility to the aspirations of American Negroes. In the following section, therefore, anti-Semitism will be defined, its extent in the black community will be examined, its anti-Jewish charges discussed, its causes probed, and various responses considered. Finally the question will be raised: Is the black American our ally or our adversary?

Chapter Eight

A NEW LOOK AT BLACK ANTI—SEMITISM

A young Afro-American stood before a Jewish audience and said: "There is no anti-Semitism in the black community." He went on to explain that anti-Semitism is prejudice based on the belief that Jews should be blamed for the death of Jesus, and blacks have no such belief. Another Afro-American stated that many Jewish teachers, merchants, and landlords deserve to be criticized, but deserved criticism is not prejudice. A Jewish member of the New Left explained that in their understandably angry mood blacks will use highly charged emotional language which should not be taken literally.

Replying to all those who would minimize anti-Jewish feeling in the black community, Earl Raab has responded that "poetic excess" is the stuff of which political anti-Semitism is made. In his provocative article, "The Black Revolution and the Jewish Question," he claimed that the "expressivism" of the new militants has given rise to an anti-Semitic ideology.[1] An increasing number of blacks (and whites) are supporting a political movement that does contain anti-Semitism in its party line, even though they, themselves, may not be hostile to Jews. The consequence of this is that political anti-Semitism has already been reintroduced "as a fashionable item in the American public arena." There is also the dangerous possibility that as the black community gains more power in the urban areas in or around which most Jews live, then—assuming the expressivist movement continues to grow—the "effect on Jewish lives will be incalculable." Jews may be pulled down so that blacks can move higher in the social structure. American foreign policy could be made less sympathetic towards Israel. Most frightening of all, the WASP class and the black mass may form a kind of alliance by means of which the Establishment would allow the blacks to move up at the expense of the Jews.

So, on the one hand, there are complete denials of
the existence of black anti-Semitism (or perhaps the con-
cession that a trace does exist but hardly warrants all the fuss
made in the Jewish community) and, on the other hand,
there is the ominous picture painted by those who see
in recent developments somber signs of the classic use
of the Jew by the ruling power as a scapegoat that the
masses might attack at will. Many Jews who believe that
anti-Semitism is running rampant in the black community have concluded: "If they hate us, why should we
lift a finger to help them?" As a guide to understanding
this complex phenomenon, this chapter will first examine
some of the charges against the Jews. Then the extent
of black anti-Semitism will be considered, its causes ana-
lyzed, and its danger weighed. Finally possible responses
will be explored.

The Evidence of Bigotry

In order to determine the existence or extent of anti-
Semitism, one must first define the term. The word,
itself, was coined in 1881 in Germany as a means of
connoting the hostility directed against Jews as an alleged
race. In contrast to the medieval anti-Jewish feeling that
was rationalized by theological preconceptions about the
role of the Jews in history, anti-Semitism was justified
by the claim that "the Jewish race" had certain undesirable characteristics and was, therefore, a danger to mankind.
Today anti-Semitism is generally considered to be simply
prejudice against Jews. This type of "ethnic prejudice"
Gordon Allport defines as:

> . . . An antipathy based upon a faulty and inflexible general-
> ization. It may be felt or expressed. It may be directed to-
> ward a group as a whole, or toward an individual because
> he is a member of that group.[2]

Because it is difficult to be certain of or to measure "anti-
pathy," a more objective definition might be: a false,
rigid, and disparaging generalization about Jews.

As an example of such a generalization, consider the statement read to the New York City's Board of Education in August, 1966, by a Melvin Pritchard:

One particular ethnic group of non-Christians are *willfully, deliberately,* and *intentionally* depriving American citizens of their right to first-class education in the community public schools of this city, state, and nation. . . . This controlling group willfully, intentionally, and deliberately administers inferior educational programs to the Christians in their community public schools . . . *the plan being to mentally murder all citizens not of their religious, racial, or ethnic group.*[3] (Emphasis added)

These remarks were greeted with sustained applause. Despite the obvious anti-Semitism clearly aimed at encouraging some white Christians to form an alliance with blacks against Jews, the white president of the Board of Education uttered not a word of public protest against this paranoid delusion. The charge that Jewish teachers as a group are committing "cultural genocide" against black children was made by John F. Hatchett and others during the Ocean Hill-Brownsville conflict in Brooklyn.[4] Attempts to drive Jewish teachers and principals out of schools in the New York area were usually accompanied by anti-Semitic remarks and occasionally by threats against the lives of Jewish school personnel. This was followed by threats against Jewish merchants. One leaflet distributed by students in December, 1968, urged disrupting "all Jew pig's businesses in your area by any means possible . . ."[5]

Bitter experiences with individual Jews who work in the black ghetto have led some blacks to make sweeping statements about Jews in general. In November, 1966, on the David Susskind television show, a black American spoke these words:

I think the majority of white Jews . . . oppress and exploit black people throughout this nation . . . They sell the bad meat to us in the markets in our ghettos. They're the lawyers who sell us out when we get in trouble. They're the ones who get my mother (involved) in time payments. They're the ones most visible.

Sometimes statements against Israel coming from SNCC and Black Panther publications are defended as "anti-Zionist" rather than "anti-Semitic." However, the line between the two is so thin as to be meaningless when false charges are leveled at the Israelis: in August, 1967, a SNCC newsletter claimed that in 1956 the Zionists lined up refugees in Gaza and shot them in the back in cold blood, and showed a cartoon of a hand marked with the Star of David and a dollar sign, tightening a rope fastened around the necks of Nasser and Cassius Clay. A month later in Chicago, at a convention of the New Left, the black delegates insisted on the adoption of certain resolutions as the price of their participation, among them, a strong statement condemning "Zionistic imperialism." The white delegates gave in to the demand. More recently in the *Black Panther* the anti-Israel line has taken the form of glorifying the Al Fatah, who deny Israel's very right to exist.[6]

To such evidence of anti-Semitism, some blacks (and whites) will respond: "But Jewish teachers, merchants, and Zionists do *deserve* to be criticized! Perhaps some critics have overstated their case but perhaps also Jews, by crying anti-Semitism, are blinding themselves to their own failings." One must be careful not to allow a defense against false generalizations to become a justification for all Jewish behavior. Let us, therefore, examine the charges leveled at the Jewish community.

The Truth about the Jews

To denounce anti-Semitism is not to claim that the Jewish community is morally pure. David Rogers, in his study of New York's predominantly Jewish educational bureaucracy, has cited evidence that there *was* a degree of discrimination against black personnel: e.g., an exaggerated emphasis on speech habits in examinations and an in-group monopoly on coaching courses for exam preparation. However, Rogers also noted that when Catholics dominated the system, other kinds of discrimination were practiced against the Jews.[7] Evidently when Jews become part of a large bureaucratic system, *some* of them will act in ways remarkably similar to the ways other people act when they find themselves in such systems. Above all, it is grossly unfair to jump from this critique of bureaucrats to the charge that thousands of Jewish teachers who have given their lives to education are purposely stifling the minds of black children.

In similar fashion, to denounce anti-Semitism is not to excuse exploitation whenever it is practiced by Jewish merchants. Professor David Caplovitz, sociologist from the University of Chicago, has reported how high-pressure salesmen (Jewish and non-Jewish) persuade the unsophisticated slum dweller to buy more expensive merchandise than he can afford, how they charge him astronomical interest rates, and how—when he can no longer pay—they turn him over to impersonal collection agencies.[8]

On behalf of the merchants, it is claimed that they are not making extraordinary profits, and Lenore Berson has shown that in Philadelphia this claim is valid.[9] Furthermore, the retailers report that because of the difficulty in collecting from slum dwellers and because of large losses due to theft, interest rates and prices must be high if any reasonable profit is to be made. Finally, many of the merchants feel compelled to remain in the ghetto. The store is often a family business, which in the previous generation had served a Jewish neighborhood. Then blacks moved into the area, and the retailer found himself in a black rather than a Jewish ghetto. Because of the great difficulties faced these days by small independent businesses, the merchant (usually an older man) may not be able to sell his business and open a new store elsewhere.

To repeat: that there are some Jewish merchants who do practice willful deception and misrepresentation is to be bitterly deplored. It is tragic that any merchant should feel compelled to engage in a business that requires high prices and interest of those who can least afford to pay. Still one should remember that Jewish businessmen in slum areas will behave about the same as non-Jewish businessmen in such areas.

It is both ironic and inconsistent for black self-determinists, following the party line of the radical left, to attack Israel as bitterly as some have done. Israel is, after all, the consequence of Jewish self-determination, as Eldridge Cleaver himself seemed to recognize when he urged the blacks to emulate Theodor Herzl. However, Cleaver, in July 1969, endorsed the views of Al Fatah who claim that justice requires the destruction of Israel, whose very existence allegedly denies basic Arab rights. The facts are, of course, that the United Nations recognized that both Arabs and Jews have deep-rooted historic claims to Palestine. The decision to divide the land between them into two autonomous states was a just way of giving to *both* peoples the opportunity for self-determination in Palestine. The tragic conflict in the Middle East has been caused primarily by the refusal of the Arabs to accept the authenticity of any nationalism in the area other than their own, despite the facts that the Jewish people were the majority in the land for 1400 years, were driven out (though a few remained in every century), and were in every generation to pray for a return. The refugee problem would never have arisen had not the Arabs attempted to destroy the Jewish state in its moment of birth. So, to glorify the Al Fatah, as some Black Panthers have done, is to endorse a fanatic chauvinism that is "for itself, alone" and that will not grant to others the same right of national self-determination that it demands for itself.

Perhaps the truth about the Jews is that they are human. The Israelis want a homeland where they can determine their own destiny just as do other national groups. American Jews have made their home in the United States. Some have been in the forefront of the struggle for civil rights; others, under pressures real or imagined, have been indifferent or even antagonistic to this struggle. These same divisions are found among every other white American religious or ethnic group.

There are those who will say that surely the *Jews* should be able to free themselves from their social conditions and rise to a higher moral level. As a people who have known persecution, *they* should be particularly sensitive to the suffering of others. Yet Gordon Allport has reported that minority groups do not necessarily show less prejudice than the majority. They may, in fact, show *more* intolerance: "We suffered; why shouldn't they?" Therefore, according to the norms of human behavior, one has no grounds for expecting a greater sensitivity to the needs of one minority group by another. Allport also states that the Jews, as a group, *do* tend to show less prejudice than the majority (perhaps because their religious tradition has tried to transform the memory of suffering into compassion for others). However, when Jews, with or without justification, feel threatened they will tend to develop the same kind of stereotypes and fears that threatened people generally hold.

The "Guilt" of Jewish Radicals and Liberals

Perhaps the most unique generalization about Jews among black self-determinists is that Jewish liberals (along with

[148]

the radicals of the thirties) bear a major share of the responsibility for the suppression of the development of black culture and the crushing of black leadership potential. Harold Cruse has charged that the Jewish members of the Communist party in the thirties, although willing and able to develop their own cultural voice (e.g., through the journal, *Jewish Life),* denounced black attempts at ethnic expression as a nationalistic deviation from Marxism.[10] Cruse, however, failed to mention that the Communist attitude towards Jewish culture was dictated not by the desires of American Jewish Communists but by a change in the party line, which, in 1934, began to move towards a united front against Hitler. The toning down of the party's traditional opposition to Jewish nationalism was part of its attempt to win support from non-Communist liberal and progressive elements (among whom were many Jews) in its struggle against facism. There was no corresponding acceptance of black ethnic development probably because—since such development was not being urged by large numbers of American Negroes—there was nothing for the party to gain by compromising with Negro nationalism. It would, therefore, seem that the party leadership in Moscow and not the Jewish Communist of the thirties was primarily responsible for whatever inconsistency appeared in attitudes towards ethnic groups.*

The Cruse thesis is more than a minor misreading of American Jewish history. It has become the prototype of the accusation that black pride and self-determination did not develop primarily because white radicals and liberals (many of whom were Jewish) took over civil rights organizations and did not allow black leadership to develop. The real reasons for this lack of ethnic development were twofold: 1) The American Negro had for over three hundred years been so brutally suppressed (and not by liberals) that the links with his ethnic heritage had been broken and his sense of self-respect had been shattered: 2) the kind of historic events that would precipitate black nationalism (as they had Jewish nationalism) had not yet occurred: *viz.,* the arousal of high hopes

---

* It is ironic that some black self-determinists, in supporting the Al Fatah, are today doing exactly what Cruse accused Jewish Communists of having done in the thirties: advocating the development of their own nationalism while denying the right of another ethnic group (in this case, the Jews) to express their own authentic national spirit. But then, projection has always played a prominent part in prejudice.

among the masses followed by their frustration. One may recall that the Russian Jewish radicals were also not allowed to develop Jewish culture within the RSDP. However, because their heritage had been fully transmitted to them, after their high hopes had been shattered, they simply formed their own proudly Jewish socialist party.

The point is that no matter what Jewish radicals or liberals would have done in the thirties, forties, or fifties, the black movement towards self-determination would not have taken place. Still, black radicals persist in singling out for blame not the bigots ("at least they are honest") but the one group that was trying to bring them into the mainstream of American life. Why? Because according to the self-determinists, integration was a false ideal. It could not come true in a racist society. This distorted line of thought would be analagous to the Jewish people blaming the *philosophes* of the French Revolution for preaching the ideals of freedom, because liberal forces in Europe were crushed by fascism.

There is, of course, an important political reason for the attack on the liberal. The greatest stumbling block before any radical movement is the liberal's persistent belief that significant social reform can take place, in this case that "the system" can be sufficiently flexible to enable all to share in its benefits. This liberal faith is today being severely tested, but most liberals cling to it, since they see the radical alternatives as leading only to chaos and repression.

There may also be psychological reasons for the bitter attacks on liberals. Bayard Rustin has explained the bitterness, in part, as an adolescent rebellion against those "who use to be loved most."[11] One can only guess at the reason behind the charge of Malcolm X that Jews were active in the Civil Rights movement so that "prejudice in America could be focused upon the Negro" rather than on the Jew.[12] Whatever Malcolm's motives, this was indeed a vicious generalization to make about thousands of Jewish liberals who believed almost as an article of faith that no minority in America can be truly free unless the rights of all minorities are secure.

Discussion: What is your opinion of the motives of liberals (Jewish and non-Jewish) in supporting the civil rights cause? What should their present role be in relation to equal rights? How do you feel about the guilt of liberals? To what extent do they share the guilt of the larger society? What more could they have done? What could they do now?

Jews often blame all the Germans for the holocaust, just as blacks often blame all whites for their suffering in America. Are such charges of group-guilt justified?—against the Germans?—against white Americans?

The Extent of Black Anti-Semitism

According to Professor Gary Marx's "study of belief in the black community," it is simply not true that blacks generally are highly anti-Semitic. Professor Marx devised an anti-Semitism index which includes three kinds of stereotypes about Jews: that they are deceitful in business, are clannish, and hold too much power. He found that approximately 30 percent of the sample of blacks in northern cities and 20 percent of those in the South scored high on the index. When the proportion of blacks who were highly anti-Semitic was compared with the proportion of whites from similar regional and educational backgrounds who were also highly anti-Semitic, they were usually found to be about the same. Whenever marked differences did appear, they seemed to cancel each other out: Northern blacks with some college education were more anti-Semitic than college-educated Northern whites—by two to one! However, Southern whites with but a grammar school background were more anti-Semitic than Southern Negroes who attended only grammar school by three to one! Judging from this 1964 survey, blacks, on balance, are no more anti-Semitic than are white non-Jews!

As for the widespread opinion that blacks have a special dislike for Jews that goes beyond their dislike for whites generally, this opinion was shown by the Marx study to be completely erroneous:

> In response to the question, "Do you think it is better to work for a Jewish person or for a white person who is not Jewish" about half the sample responded "the same" or "don't know." But the remainder of the sample was much more likely to favor a Jewish employer over a non-Jewish one, particularly in New York City (36 to 19 percent), Atlanta (36 to 16 percent), and Birmingham (35 to 15 percent). [13]

Regarding Jewish or white non-Jewish merchants and land-lords, about seven out of ten in the sample did not indicate any preference, but of those who did, Jews were favored: In New York, Jewish merchants barely favored by 10 to 7, but landlords by 19 to 11; in Chicago, merchants by 15 to 8 and landlords, 22 to 7; in Atlanta, merchants by 32 to 4 and landlords, 31 to 4! Evidently, blacks insofar as they have a preference, tend to choose to have business contacts with Jewish rather than non-Jewish whites.

These findings, however encouraging, raise a problem: If blacks are no more anti-Semitic towards Jews than are white non-Jews, and if blacks in some cases even prefer contacts with Jews rather than with white non-Jews,— then how can one account for the deep-rooted conviction of so many Jews that "Negroes don't like us no matter what the statistics show?" The answer may lie in the fact, *that the study dealt with biased attitudes, not with public expression of prejudice.* Black anti-Semites undoubtedly express their prejudiced attitudes more openly in word and deed than do white anti-Semites. In white America, it is simply not respectable publicly to give vent to anti-Semitic feelings. (The John Birch Society, for example, has denied that it has anything against Jews.) However, within the black community there is so much frustration that anti-Semitic Negroes may feel comparatively less in-hibited about openly voicing and acting out their prejudices. One should not be surprised that Jews who rarely encounter outspoken hostility from white non-Jews are shocked and shaken when they hear rude remarks and angry accusations coming from customers in their stores or classmates in their schools.

Nathan Glazer suspects that such studies, made in 1964, do not reflect Negro opinion today.* What is im-portant, in his view, is "not so much the general level of anti-Semitic feeling in the ghetto as the dramatic increase in expressions of anti-Semitism among some . . . black leaders."[14] Earl Raab considers such studies to be ir-relevant, since anti-Semitism has become part of a political

* However, the *Newsweek* Poll (Report from Black America) reported on June 30, 1969, that "Jews are rated favorably (by blacks) by 2 to 1 and *actually fare better than whites generally.*" (Emphasis added) the implica-tion is that the statistics of the Marx study of 1964 pertaining to the atti-tudes of Negroes towards Jews could still be considered a valid reflection of Negro opinion five years later.

movement that is supported by many who are not hostile to Jews. This raises the question of the threat posed by black anti-Semitism, be it politically, economically, or psychologically motivated. How serious one considers the threat will depend upon how one interprets the causes.

Sources of Black Anti-Semitism

1. Frequent Contacts with Jewish Businessmen

As has been stated, a high proportion of the merchants, landlords, and pawnbrokers with whom the black slum-dweller deals are Jewish. Professor Marx found that those Negroes who have had frequent contacts with Jewish businessmen were much more likely to be anti-Semitic than those who have not had such contacts. Evidently there is something about depending on and feeling subordinate to another person (whether merchant or landlord) that encourages resentment. Among those who, as a result of such dealings, felt that Jewish store owners had treated them unfairly, 70 percent were highly anti-Semitic! The charges made against merchants in the ghetto and their justifications for certain practices have been discussed. Whatever may be one's judgment, the very fact of frequent contacts and the widespread impression of exploitation are significant sources of black anti-Semitism.

2. Indoctrination in Fundamentalist Christianity

Rabbi Robert Gordis has maintained that there is a significant religious factor in black anti-Semitism. As he has explained:

> When the American Negro was kidnaped from his native Africa and brought to the United States and cast into slavery, he was converted to Christianity in its most literalistic form. Lacking the education and sophistication which even his white masters rarely possessed he could hardly be expected to counter the outspoken anti-Jewish bias of the Gospels. He therefore tended to identify the Jew, whom he knew from the New Testament, with the enemy of God.[15]

On the other hand, James Baldwin, whose father was a fundamentalist preacher, has maintained that in black churches the image of the Jew as Christ-killer is not created nearly so vividly as is the image of the Jew as slave, with whom the "Old Testament oriented" Negro easily identifies.[16] Despite the centrality of the crucifixion story in the Negro Evangelical Church, there is less evidence of an anti-Jewish bias there than in white fundamentalist churches. The Negro singing "Go Down Moses" seems less likely than white Christian fundamentalists to think of Jews as "the enemy of God."

It would seem, therefore, that Fundamentalist Christianity could either plant the seed of religious bigotry or develop an image of the Jew to which the Negro might favorably respond . . . or both.

3. Jewish Suffering As a Factor in Black Anti-Semitism

Being aware that Jews have been oppressed through history does not necessarily mean that blacks will feel more kindly towards them today. Baldwin has gone so far as to write, "The Jew does not realize that the fact he has been despised and slaughtered does not increase the Negro's understanding. It increases the Negro's rage."[17] How so? Because the Jew was persecuted, the Negro expects *more* understanding from him than from the non-Jew. So, when a Jew behaves as any other white man, the black man becomes particularly resentful. The Jew, who should know the meaning of oppression, has not lived up to expectations. That this expectation is not lived up to by minority groups in general has already been noted.

Another reason that the history of Jewish suffering may indirectly contribute to black anti-Semitism is that the American Jew is *no longer* suffering. *He* has prospered in "the Promised Land," and according to Bayard Rustin, the disadvantaged Negro deeply resents anyone who has escaped the poverty that is still his lot:

> . . . The Negro holds the greatest disrespect for those who have made it when he has nothing. I've made it, James Farmer has made it, Martin Luther King has made it. But there is nobody who has made it more than the Jews, and nobody who started more handicapped.[18]

4. The Need to Belong

It has often been suggested that to be anti-Semitic is one way for the Negro to have the illusion that he is part of the American mainstream. That is, by adopting a prejudice that is held by a significant number of those in the majority group (white Gentile), he may, in some sense, feel that he "belongs." In January 1969, a sixteen-year-old Negro girl wrote in the introduction to a catalogue for a "Harlem on My Mind" exhibit at the Metropolitan Museum of Art: ". . . blacks may find that anti-Jewish sentiments place them, for once, in the majority." (Mayor Lindsay deplored anti-Jewish accusations in the introduction, but despite many protests, the catalogue was not withdrawn from circulation.)

5. Economic and Political Factors

Most analysts, while recognizing the significance of the above factors, consider as even more important certain political forces and economic conditions that make the Jew a natural target for the frustrations of blacks who are blocked in their attempts to become part of the mainstream of American life. However, the precise nature of these forces and conditions and the manner of their interaction are subjects of considerable controversy.

a. The Scapegoat Theory
According to this view, by attacking the Jew, the Negro is (1) expressing his hatred for the entire white community and (2) diverting his anger and energy away from the source of his trouble and on to the most convenient target, or scapegoat. As James Baldwin has written:

> The Negro, facing the Jew, hates, at bottom, not his Jewishness but the color of his skin . . . Just as a society must have a scapegoat so hatred must have a symbol. Georgia has its Negro and Harlem has the Jew.[19]

Baldwin noted a parallel between anti-Semitism in Harlem and the persecution of the medieval Jew who was often a businessman or money lender dealing with the under-privileged. In both situations, hatred of the Jew diverted the masses from the basic causes of their misery. On resigning from the staff of the black nationalist magazine,

[155]

Liberator, after it had run a series of anti-Semitic articles, Baldwin wrote:

> I think it is distinctly unhelpful, and I think it is immoral to blame Harlem on the Jew . . . Why, when we should be storming capitols, do you suggest to the people you hope to serve that they take refuge in the most ancient and barbaric of European myths . . .

In a subsequent article for *The New York Times,* he continued in the same vein: "(The Jew) is playing in Harlem the role assigned him by Christians long ago: He is doing their dirty work."[20]

b. "The People in Between"

Rabbi Robert J. Marx has gone beyond the scapegoat theory in his view of the Jewish community as "interstitial . . . located between the parts of the social structure of western societies. Neither part of the masses nor of the power structure, Jews wereuniquely positioned so that they fulfilled certain vital, yet dispensable functions, for the society of which they were a part." For example, Ukranian Jews in the seventeenth century were caught, in the words of Simon Dubnow:

> . . . between hammer and anvil; between the pan (feudal lord) and the Khlopf (peasant), between the Catholic and the Greek Orthodox, between the Pole and the Russian.

This meant that they were vulnerable to attack from *both* the angry masses and the rulers trying to preserve their power.

So today, according to Rabbi Marx, Jewish merchants, builders, and teachers are interstitial and, therefore, vulnerable to prejudice from blacks and to subtle manipulation by the power structure. However, too much energy is "spent agonizing over black anti-Semitism," since "anti-Semitism on the part of a minority group is not nearly as dangerous as when a majority group seizes upon it as a way of maintaining its power."[21] He fears that the white power structure could respond in this way to Negro social unrest, especially should there be a prolonged depression.

c. Anti-Semitism as Political Ideology

Earl Raab, also viewing the Jew as interstitial and hence vulnerable to attack from both sides, has warned the community that the danger is very real: Anti-Semitism has become part of the ideology of black expressivism. It poses a serious threat, because that ideology might gain the support of the masses of not necessarily anti-Semitic people and its spokesmen, having gained power, could take actions detrimental to Jews. Imagine what would happen if black militants took over the leadership of the great urban centers! For Raab, the Jewish community is in danger both from the power structure and from the emerging black community:

> There is the possibility of a classic marriage, a manipulative symbiosis, between the privileged class and the dis-privileged mass—in this case a WASP class and a black mass . . . [22]

d. Critique of Interstitial-Political Interpretations
Nathan Glazer has been critical of the Raab thesis on a number of counts. The fear that the black community might elect urban leaders who would take actions against the Jews is unrealistic: "of all the anti-Semitic statements which have recently been publicized by the mass media, not a single one has come from an elected representative of the black community."[23] That is, when all the elements in the black community have chosen government officials, they have usually elected responsible leaders.

No real damage could be done to the Jewish community without the cooperation of the white Establishment, where the decisive power lies, no matter who might have been elected mayor. Glazer comments that the Jews are much more a part of the Establishment than they themselves generally recognize. Most important, despite all the accusations of late, the Establishment has *not* singled out the Jewish community *as a whole* as a scapegoat that blacks might attack with impunity:

> . . . if the Establishment has acted to sacrifice the interest of the lower-middle-class Jewish teachers in New York to black militants in the hope of achieving civic peace, it has acted in exactly the same way with regard to the interests *of all working-class and lower-middle-class groups, Jewish and non-Jewish alike.*[24] (Emphasis added)

It is crucial to note that the vast majority of the Jewish community, engaged in business or professions that serve the public-at-large, have not been victimized by either the white power structure or the black community. Therefore, one may question whether Jews, as Jews or as a total community, are so seriously threatened as the interstitial-political interpretations imply.

e. The Problem of Succession

The conflict between blacks and Jews in New York City has been widely interpreted as an outgrowth of "succession, the process by which members of one ethnic or racial group . . . move up a notch on the socio-economic ladder and are succeeded in their old position by a less affluent group."[25] In New York, the problem was that as the less affluent group (the blacks) attempted to move up into the educational profession, those Jews who had dominated the profession did not "move up a notch" but wanted to retain their old position. The conflict, then, was not essentially between all-blacks and all-Jews but between poor blacks and sub-affluent Jews. It was inevitable that this tension would give rise to anti-Semitism and anti-Negro expressions on the respective sides.

This interpretation does explain the particular virulence of the conflict in New York City. However, in cities where blacks are not trying to enter occupational areas dominated by Jews, anti-Semitism is still expressed: the Jewish merchant and landlord being vulnerable targets for the rage of the slum dweller, who attacks them as symbols of the system. Still, insofar as the succession-process is a major factor, the danger posed would seem to be limited primarily to those specific Jews who are trying to retain their occupational positions despite the rise of a new ethnic group. Herbert Gans has suggested that in New York "this is presumably why major Jewish organizations dominated by upper middle-class Jews did not take a stand on the union cause."[26]

6. Light from the Jewish Past

A distinction between two types of European anti-Semitism might shed some light on black anti-Semitism as well as on the various theories advanced to explain it. Jews have been used by those in power to protect their own position: e.g., the feudal nobility and church would direct the antagonism of the masses against the Jews in order to preserve the status quo and their own place in the power structure. On the other hand, Jews have been used *not* by the "ins" but by the "outs" to stir up the masses *against the existing government.* In this type of "outgroup anti-Semitism" the Jew was often identified with the Establishment by those who wished to pull them both down: e.g., the Dreyfus Case, in which the attack on Dreyfus by the church, army, and royalists was, in effect, an attack on the Third Republic. A closer historic parallel to the anti-Semitism in the dark ghetto was the "out-group anti-Semitism" found among some European socialists of the nineteenth century.

In France, Charles Fourier had a bitter hatred of commerce and of the Jew, who represented to him the mercantile spirit. The socialist Proudhon identified the Jew with the power of the Rothchilds and so viewed him as the enemy of social revolution. Karl Marx, born of Jewish parents who had converted to Christianity, attacked the Jewish people as the personification of capitalism. Other socialist leaders, being rational enough to realize that the system they opposed was neither created nor controlled by Jews, were not anti-Semitic. Still, it is an uncanny echo of history to hear the small group of black revolutionaries who talk most freely of shattering the entire social system, invoke once again the image of the evil power of the Jewish capitalist.

It would seem that black anti-Semitism today bears a greater resemblence to the out-group than the in-group variety. The main instigators are extremists in the black community *who are just as bitter towards the Establishment as they are towards the Jews.* In fact, the study of Professor Marx showed that 96 percent of highly anti-Semitic Negroes were also highly anti-white. This suggested to Professor Marx that black anti-Semitism is *not* a diversion of hostility *away from* the white community. Could it be, instead, part of the antagonism directed against whites, in general? One could still consider anti-Semitism to be based on a scapegoat mechanism in that it diverts the attention of the black not from "whitey" but from those basic social, economic, and political efforts that must be made before true equality is to be achieved. Glazer also has maintained that anti-Semitism should be viewed in the context of the more general trend towards more open and extreme anti-white expressions in the black community.[27]

If it be true that black anti-Semitism is an integral part of an attack against the white community, then the Establishment might be expected to recognize that the more revolutionary self-determinists will not be distracted from their goals of fundamental changes in society by Jew-baiting. The city fathers may not protect those Jewish *and non-Jewish whites* working in occupational areas that some blacks are trying to enter. However, this is a far cry from the picture of WASP leaders directing black power against the Jewish community *in general.* In the past the power structure has often defended the Jews against out-groups that used anti-Semitism in their attack on the system: e.g., the Third Republic backed Dreyfus against the army and Royalists. One would hope that the "power elite" today would oppose any anti-Semitism serving a similar political function.

Jewish history does indicate that there is one set of conditions under which those in power might be tempted to hold the Jew out as scapegoat for the frustrated and oppressed: Should the American economy and its political system truly be on the verge of collapse, then to save their power, certain leaders might resort to totalitarian control. Under such a neo-fascism, all minorities would be repressed and could be turned against one another. One would hope that since the Keynesian Revolution in economic thought, it is now possible through proper fiscal policies and wise use of the public sector of the economy to prevent a chronic depression.

That there seems little likelihood of catastrophe is not a reason for dismissing the anti-Semitism that does exist. As the movement towards black self-determination develops, the more vulnerable members of the Jewish community (e.g., merchants and teachers in the inner city) will be threatened. The overall picture, then, gives cause for neither complacency nor panic. Black anti-Semitism does exist. It is directed from within the black community primarily against those Jews who work within the ghetto and who seem to stand in the way of upwardly mobile blacks. The danger to the Jewish community as a whole either from black demogogues or white manipulators has perhaps been exaggerated.

Discussion: How much of a threat do you consider black anti-Semitism to be? Should Jews be concerned with "mere words," as opposed to harmful acts? Which groups within the Jewish community do you believe are threatened? Is there a real danger that black militants might take over the great American cities? Would the entire Jewish community then be in trouble? How great is the danger of a chronic depression in the United States? What would be its effect on American Jews? What effect do you think the attitude of black militants towards Israel might have on United States policy in the Middle East? Why might some black self-determinists

[160]

have mixed feelings about Israel? What should be the responsibility of upper middle-class Jews for sub-affluent Jews who feel threatened by blacks striving for power?

Responses to Black Anti-Semitism

1. "I Wouldn't Lift a Finger to Help Those Anti-Semites"

The impulse to react to bigotry within the black community by dropping out of (if one was ever in) the movement for truly equal opportunity is tempting. Not only is the hostility of some blacks enough to turn many away from the struggle for social justice, but now the self-determinists seem to be saying: "We don't need your help. We'd rather do it ourselves." So why should one go where he is not wanted?

Several reminders are in order before one evaluates this view. Recall that according to the Marx study only a minority of blacks are highly anti-Semitic, about the same proportion, on balance, that is found in the white community. Despite the more candid expression of feelings among blacks, should Jews withhold support from the legitimate demands of blacks because of the attitudes of a minority? Would one be justified in withholding a contribution from the United Fund because a minority of white non-Jews are anti-Semitic?

Recall also that the newer black leaders are *not* telling the white community to drop out of the struggle for social justice. They are actually saying: "Let us run our own movement. You have enough to do to combat racism in white society."

Recall, finally, that black anti-Semitism is reactive, that is, is part of the rage-reaction against the indifference and hostility of a large portion of the white (Jewish and non-Jewish) community. Remember that the Jews, when oppressed, also reacted to the outside world with suspicion and hostility. The use of black anti-Semitism as a reason for indifference to the struggle for social justice reminds one of the way some Christians used the reactive antagonism of Jews towards *goyim* as an excuse for withholding the benefits of emancipation. Assuming that some prejudice is found in every group, consider the consequence of the philosophy that says: "I won't help them because some of them don't like us."

[161]

2. A Positive Jewish Presence in the Ghetto

According to Rabbi Robert Marx, such a presence can be helpful both to blacks and Jews. In a number of urban areas, including Boston, Chicago, and Philadelphia, rabbis have become available as mediators between blacks who have complaints and merchants or landlords who are allegedly being exploitive.[28] In one case, a mortgage company that had begun foreclosure proceedings because the owner due to illness was two months behind in his payments was persuaded to work out a mutually satisfactory arrangement that would enable the owner to retain his home. Some have suggested that the Jewish community provide loans to make it possible for blacks to go into business for themselves. In Chicago, under Rabbi Marx's leadership, the Jewish Council on Urban Affairs was established to enable the Jewish community to realize the constructive possibilities of its interstitial role. The program of the JCUA includes: identifying the needs of the disinherited and interpreting those needs to the Jewish community, opposing forms of aid that weaken the recipient and develop patterns of dependency, supporting community organizations that seek to help people help themselves, going where invited to go as partners, opposing racial and religious prejudices, challenging "the Jewish community to utilize their skills, their traditions, and their commitments, to creatively bring together the fragmented parts of a society into a unity that a people of God can symbolize."

3. Leave the Ghetto

Rabbi Harold Schulweiss, in an indignant article, "The Voice of Esau," has demanded that Jewish businessmen simply *get out* of the slums. Citing rabbinic tradition to demonstrate that no Jew, whatever the circumstances, should practice *genevat daat* (stealth of mind) or *onaat d'varim* (oppression by words), he has claimed that Jewish merchants are doing just this. If it is true that in order to make a reasonable profit, they must charge high prices and interest rates, then rather than do so, they should sell their businesses and work elsewhere. No Jew should live off the misery of the poor.[29] In view of the tremendous difficulties involved in starting a new business, especially if one is no longer young, some have suggested that the Jewish community subsidize those Jewish merchants who wish to leave the ghetto. What do you think?

4. Eliminate the Sources of Frustration

If it is true, as many would agree, that the basic cause of Negro anti-Semitism is the accumulation of resentment and rage which are often directed against the most visible target (namely, the Jew) then the basic remedy would seem to be: eliminate the causes of that resentment and rage, those conditions that make it almost impossible for the child of the ghetto to enter the mainstream of American life. Whether one holds to Baldwin's version of the scapegoat theory (the black man hates at bottom the color of the Jew's skin), or to the concept of interstitiality (that the Jew is vulnerable from both sides), or to Raab's view of political ideology as the major threat, or to the out-group thesis that sees anti-Semitism as part of an attack on the system as a whole—whatever one's interpretation of political and economic factors, at the root of the prejudice is still the anger that comes from being excluded from the benefits that are more readily available to white Americans. Therefore, it is actually in the self-interest of the Jewish community to work for the day when blacks will no longer be so stifled by conditions that are the consequence of centuries of injustice. Should America channel but a portion of the funds that have gone (or will go) into the Vietnam war, the anti-ballistics missile system, and the space program into a multi-faceted national effort for housing, education, and employment, then the poor, both black and white, would find that America is, indeed, a land of opportunity, and the frustration that underlies anti-Semitism would be greatly relieved. The ultimate answer to bigotry can only be a society that does not stifle its members so that they strike out at the most convenient target.

5. "Reinvigorate the Succession Process"

Attacking poverty is not enough if, when blacks rise into various occupations, they must enter into a bitter conflict with the "sub-affluent." Therefore, Herbert Gans has written that "the time has come . . . to reinvigorate the succession process" by using public funds "to create jobs in the professional, semi-professional, and technical occupations that would allow both the sub-affluent and the poor to move up in the economic hierarchy."[30] With the great need for more people in the educational profession, as well as in other occupations that provide services to people, such a program would be of benefit to the community as a whole.

6. The Moral Imperative: Be Guided by Moral Values, Not Negro Attitudes

A Jew's concern with social justice should have nothing whatsoever to do with how many Negroes like or dislike the Jewish people. This was the point made by Charles Silberman in an address before the American Jewish Congress:

> . . . anti-Semitism is irrelevent to a consideration of Jewish responsibility because, in the most fundamental sense, that responsibility stems from us and not from Negroes. As the Synagogue Council of America has put it, "As Jews, we are committed by our faith to work for racial justice in an integrated society. Any Jew who fails to join in this struggle demeans his faith." What we do, in other words—what we are *obliged* to do—we are obliged to do not because of Negroes . . . not because of what Negroes do or don't do, not because of what Negroes are or are not—but because of what we are ourselves, because of our obligation, in the prophetic injunction, to do justice. And the injunction is to *do* justice; justice is an act, not a state of mind. We must become involved in the fight for racial justice, in other words, not because Negroes are deserving objects of our benevolence, but simply because it is the right thing to do.[31]

But might not striving for justice for blacks mean opposing the interests of the Jewish community? If justice for blacks should call for eliminating the shameful conditions that give rise to the frustration at the root of bigotry, then such justice would indeed be for the well-being of the Jew as well as the black. That is to say, creating a world where Jews can be secure *means* creating a world where all men can have the opportunity for self-fulfillment. Recalling the words of Deutero-Isaiah, caring for "the offspring of Israel" actually implies being a "light unto the nations!"

[164]

However, it is easier to talk about pursuing justice for Jew and non-Jew alike than to do it, especially if one has in fact, experienced the hostility of the black man. It would be helpful if, despite one's natural tendency to respond in kind, he could try to listen to what the angry black is really saying. Whatever his words, his heart may well be shrieking:

> I hate being black in America. I hate sending my children to schools where they learn that they are hopelessly behind the whites on the other side of town. I hate seeing my children go out into streets where the heroes are the hustlers who make their living stealing, whoring or selling pot. I hate being turned down for jobs I can handle. I hate thinking of thousands of young men who have nothing to look forward to but menial work at miserable wages. And I hate being told after everything that's been done for us for over three hundred years, that we should be able by just a little more effort to live the good life.

When some of this hatred is, for whatever combination of reasons, directed towards Jews, we then have a choice. We may "hate back" or we may consider the causes of hatred and what to do about them.

Discussion: Of all the responses in the preceding section, which make the most sense to you? Does justice for the black mean to you: a) supporting no anti-poverty program on the theory that "enough has been done for them"; b) advocating a more massive effort to eliminate slum conditions; c) opposing all efforts by blacks to gain a larger share of power over their own community's institutions; d) favoring all efforts towards black community control?

Allies or Adversaries

Are blacks and Jews allies or adversaries? The answer is not a simple one. There will always be some Jews who so ardently identify with the cause of black nationalism that they look the other way when some Negro demagogue attacks their own Jewish community. In a column cleverly critical of this Jewish Uncle Tom, M. Jay Rosenberg has written that "he, not today's black, is the invisible man; he, like yesterday's Negro, wanders in a no man's land," as he denies his heritage while hailing black culture.[32] In contrast to this Uncle Tom, a Jew who has respect for himself and his heritage will not fail to speak out against the anti-Semitic bigot, even though he be black.

At the same time, the Jew who appreciates the value of his own culture, will understand why it is important for blacks to develop pride in their own heritage and to achieve a share of the power that all groups seek in American life. The difficulty arises when the claim for a share of power becomes a demand that denies to others certain basic human rights. It is not easy always to ascertain just when this line is crossed. There may well be a tendency on the part of threatened Jews to exaggerate the danger, just as there will be a tendency on the part of blacks to claim that they are threatening no one's legitimate rights. One would hope that this process of accommodation will take place in a spirit of mutual respect and sensitivity.

Finally, there is a deeper sense in which the answer to the question, "Allies or Adversaries?" is not in doubt. Both groups are dependent for their well-being, on a society that provides to all of its members the opportunity for self-fulfillment. Perhaps for the first time in human history, technology has developed to the point where such a society is possible; the United States has the resources to enable all its people to be free to be themselves. Whether or not these resources will be so employed is another question. We in America face a choice as old as Israel. May we hearken to the biblical command: "Choose life, that thou mayest live, thou and thy seed . . . "[33]

EPILOGUE

What, then, is "A Jewish view of the Black Revolution"? It is learning to see with our minds and with our hearts. It is looking at the culture of poverty and asking why? It is rejecting the doctrine of inherent racial inferiority when such a doctrine can be shown to be fallacious. It is trying to understand what combination of conditions can produce the kind of frustration and despair that explodes into violence. It is studying the economic feasibility of a freedom budget and examining the verbal achievement tests of children in integrated classrooms. It is recognizing that seeing with mind, alone, is not enough.

"A Jewish View" is looking into our neighbor's heart and finding a human being who has the same yearnings that we have. It is seeing the world from his perspective and trying to understand what gives him pain. It is examining our fundamental values and asking ourselves why we believe in them. It is confronting conflicts between our ideals and other less noble but equally compelling desires . . . or even between one ideal and another. It is sometimes asking ourselves how much we should give up for the sake of our neighbor.

Finally, "A Jewish View" is asking all these questions in the light of Jewish belief and experience. It it becoming aware that in Judaism there are various theological doctrines, all of which imply that we should care about the rights of our fellowmen. It is realizing that our faith has attempted to transform the memory of Jewish suffering into compassion for the suffering of all victims of oppression. It is understanding how Jewish law has reflected the conditions of life each generation, at times falling short of the goal of human equality. It is choosing to strive for the achievement of that goal despite the conditions of our time. It is the refusal to use Jewish history to justify indifference to injustice. Above all, it is the willingness to consult the collective wisdom of our heritage to discover those insights and ideals that might illumine our way.

APPENDIX I

Chronology of the "Negro Revolt"

1941: After a threatened march on Washington, President Roosevelt bans discrimination in defense industries.

1954: Supreme Court rules against compulsory segregation in state-supported elementary and secondary schools.

1955: Montgomery Bus Boycott launches the Civil Rights movement.

1957: Congress passes the first Civil Rights Bill in 82 years, and President Eisenhower sends troops to Little Rock to enforce integration.

1959: Supreme Court declares unconstitutional the massive resistance (closing of public school system) of some Virginia districts.

1960: Sit-ins in the South open lunch counters to Negroes in scores of cities.

1961: "Freedom Riders" go south to desegregate interstate bus terminals. Interstate Commerce Commission ends all segregation in such facilities.

1962: James Meredith admitted to University of Mississippi despite resistance of Governor Barnett and violence on campus.

1963: Negroes of Birmingham demand both desegregation and employment opportunity. Reverend King and others jailed for civil disobedience. Bull Conner's police dogs shock nation. Civic leaders come to terms, but four girls killed by bomb thrown into Negro church. In Jackson, Mississippi, Medgar Evers, civil rights worker, is fatally shot.

210,000 whites and Negroes march on Washington to urge passage of major Civil Rights Bill.

1964: Civil Rights Act of 1964 bans discrimination in places of public accommodations, desegregates public facilities, prohibits discrimination by most employers and labor unions, encourages school desegregation.

COFO Summer: Students go to Mississippi to teach in freedom schools and encourage voter registration. Andrew Goodman, James Chaney, and Michael Schwerner murdered.

Riots in Harlem, Brooklyn, Rochester, and Philadelphia.

President Johnson signs Economic Opportunity Act, launching war against poverty.

1965: March from Selma to Montgomery to petition for the right to vote turned back. Reverend James J. Reeb killed. March takes place. Mrs. Viola Liuzzo murdered.

Civil Rights Act of 1965 guarantees Negroes the right to vote.

"Insurrection" in Watts section of Los Angeles.

1966: Riots in Chicago and Cleveland.

1967: Riots in more than a score of cities, including Cincinnati, Atlanta, Buffalo, and Newark.

Most destructive explosion thus far in Detroit.

1968: Murder of Rev. Martin Luther King. Passage of Civil Rights Act with fair housing provision.

APPENDIX II: ON CIVIL DISOBEDIENCE

A Statement by Eight Alabama Clergymen
and Excerpts from the Response by
Reverend Martin Luther King, Jr.
(plus a portion of Rev. King's March on
Washington address of August, 1963)

*The following is the public statement directed to Martin
Luther King, Jr., by eight Alabama clergymen.*

"We the undersigned clergymen are among those who, in
January, issued 'An Appeal for Law and Order and Common
Sense,' in dealing with racial problems in Alabama. We expressed understanding that honest convictions in racial matters could properly be pursued in the courts, but urged that
decisions of those courts should in the meantime be peacefully obeyed.

"Since that time there had been some evidence of increased forbearance and a willingness to face facts. Responsible citizens have undertaken to work on various problems
which cause racial friction and unrest. In Birmingham, recent public events have given indication that we all have opportunity for a new constructive and realistic approach to
racial problems.

"However, we are now confronted by a series of
demonstrations by some of our Negro citizens, directed and
led in part by outsiders. We recognize the natural impatience
of people who feel that their hopes are slow in being realized.
But we are convinced that these demonstrations are unwise
and untimely.

"We agree rather with certain local Negro leadership
which has called for honest and open negotiation of racial
issues in our area. And we believe this kind of facing of
issues can best be accomplished by citizens of our own metropolitan area, white and Negro, meeting with their knowledge
and experience of the local situation. All of us need to face

that responsibility and find proper channels for its accomplishment.

"Just as we formerly pointed out that 'hatred and violence have no sanction in our religious and political traditions,' we also point out that such actions as incite to hatred and violence, however technically peaceful those actions may be, have not contributed to the resolution of our local problems. We do not believe that these days of new hope are days when extreme measures are justified in Birmingham.

"We commend the community as a whole, and the local news media and law enforcement officials in particular, on the calm manner in which these demonstrations have been handled. We urge the public to continue to show restraint should the demonstrations continue, and the law enforcement officials to remain calm and continue to protect our city from violence.

"We further strongly urge our own Negro community to withdraw support from these demonstrations, and to unite locally in working peacefully for a better Birmingham. When rights are consistently denied, a cause should be pressed in the courts and in negotiations among local leaders, and not in the streets. We appeal to both our white and Negro citizenry to observe the principles of law and order and common sense."

Bishop C. C. J. Carpenter, Bishop Joseph A. Durick, Rabbi Milton L. Grafman, Bishop Paul Hardin, Bishop Nolan B. Harmon, Rev. George M. Murray, Rev. Edward V. Ramage, Rev. Earl Stallings. *April 12, 1963*

My dear Fellow Clergymen,

While confined here in the Birmingham City Jail, I came across your recent statement calling our present activities "unwise and untimely." Frankly, I have never yet engaged in a direct action movement that was "well-timed," according to the timetable of those who have not suffered unduly from the disease of segregation. For years now I have heard the word "Wait!" It rings in the ear of every Negro with a piercing familiarity. This "Wait" has almost always meant "Never." It has been a tranquilizing thalidomide, relieving the emotional stress for a moment, only to give birth to an ill-formed infant of frustration. We must come to see with the distinguished jurist of yesterday that "justice too long delayed is justice denied." We have waited for more than three hundred and forty years for our constitutional and God-given rights. The nations of Asia and Africa are moving with jet-like speed toward the goal of political independence, and we still creep at horse and buggy pace toward the gaining of a cup of coffee at a lunch counter. I guess it is easy for those who have never felt the stinging darts of segregation to say, "Wait." But when you have seen vicious mobs lynch your mothers and fathers at will and drown your sisters and brothers at whim; when you have seen hate filled policemen curse, kick, brutalize, and even kill your black brothers and sisters with impunity; when you see the vast majority of your twenty million Negro brothers smothering in an airtight cage of poverty in the midst of an affluent society; when you suddenly find your tongue twisted and your speech stammering as you seek to explain to your six-year-old daughter why she can't go to the public amusement park that has just been advertised on television, and see tears welling up in her little eyes when she is told that Funtown is closed to colored children, and see the depressing clouds of inferiority begin to form in her little mental sky, and see her begin to distort her little personality by unconsciously developing a bitterness towards white people; when you have to concoct an answer for a five-year-old son asking in agonizing pathos: "Daddy, why do white people treat colored people so mean?"; when you take a cross country drive and find it necessary to sleep night after night in the uncomfortable corners of your automobile because no motel will accept you; when you are humiliated day in and day out by nagging signs reading "white" and "colored"; when your first name becomes "nigger" and your middle name becomes "boy" (however old you are) and your last name becomes "John," and when your wife and mother are never given the respected title "Mrs."; when you are harried by day and haunted at night by the fact that you are a Negro, living constantly at tip-toe stance never quite knowing what to expect next, and plagued with inner fears and outer resentments; when you are forever fighting a degenerating sense of "nobodiness"; then you will understand why we find it difficult to wait. There comes a time when the cup of endurance runs over, and men are no longer willing to be plunged into an abyss of injustice where they experience the blackness of corroding despair. I hope, sirs, you can understand our legitimate and unavoidable impatience.

You express a great deal of anxiety over our willingness to break laws. This is certainly a legitimate concern. Since we so diligently urge people to obey the Supreme Court's decision of 1954 outlawing segregation in the public schools, it is rather strange and paradoxical to find us consciously breaking laws. One may well ask, "How can you advocate breaking some laws and obeying others?" The answer is found in the fact that there are two types of laws: There are *just* and there are *unjust* laws. I would agree with Saint Augustine that "An unjust law is no law at all."

Now what is the difference between the two? How does one determine when a law is just or unjust? A just law is a man-made code that squares with the moral law or the law of God. An unjust law is a code that is out of harmony with the moral law. To put it in the terms of Saint Thomas Aquinas, an unjust law is a human law that is not rooted in eternal and natural law. Any law that uplifts human personality is just. Any law that degrades human personality is unjust. All segregation statutes are unjust because segregation distorts the soul and damages the personality. It gives the segregator a false sense of superiority, and the segregated a false sense of inferiority. To use the words of Martin Buber, the great Jewish philosopher, segregation substitutes an "I-it" relationship, for the "I-thou" relationship, and ends up relegating persons to the status of things. So segregation is not only politically, economically and sociologically unsound, but it is morally wrong and sinful. Paul Tillich has said that sin is separation. Isn't segregation an existential expression of man's tragic separation, an expression of his awful estrangement, his terrible sinfulness? So I can urge men to disobey segregation ordinances because they are morally wrong.

Let us turn to a more concrete example of just and unjust laws. An unjust law is a code that a majority inflicts on a minority that is not binding on itself. This is difference made legal. On the other hand a just law is a code that a majority compels a minority to follow that it is willing to follow itself. This is sameness made legal.

Let me give another explanation. An unjust law is a code inflicted upon a minority which that minority had no part in enacting or creating because they did not have the unhampered right to vote. Who can say that the legislature of Alabama which set up the segregation laws was democratically elected? Throughout the state of Alabama all types of conniving methods are used to prevent Negroes from becoming registered voters and there are some counties without a single Negro registered to vote despite the fact that the Negro constitutes a majority of the population. Can any law set up in such a state be considered democratically structured?

These are just a few examples of unjust and just laws. There are some instances when a law is just on its face and unjust in its application. For instance, I was arrested Friday on a charge of parading without a permit. Now there is nothing wrong with an ordinance which requires a permit for a parade, but when the ordinance is used to preserve segregation and to deny citizens the First Amendment privilege of peaceful assembly and peaceful protest, then it becomes unjust.

I hope you can see the distinction I am trying to point out. In no sense do I advocate evading or defying the law as the rabid segregationist would do. This would lead to anarchy. One who breaks an unjust law must do it *openly, lovingly* (not hatefully as the white mothers did in New Orleans when they were seen on television screaming "nigger, nigger, nigger") and with a willingness to accept the penalty. I submit that an individual who breaks a law that conscience tells him is unjust, and willingly accepts the penalty by staying in jail to arouse the conscience of the community over its injustice, is in reality expressing the very highest respect for law.

Of course, there is nothing new about this kind of civil disobedience. It was seen sublimely in the refusal of Shadrach, Meshach, and Abednego to obey the laws of Nebuchadnezzar because a higher moral law was involved. It was practiced superbly by the early Christians who were willing to face hungry lions and the excruciating pain of chopping blocks, before submitting to certain unjust laws of the Roman empire. To a degree academic freedom is a reality today because Socrates practiced civil disobedience.

We can never forget that everything Hitler did in Germany was "legal" and everything the Hungarian freedom fighters did in Hungary was "illegal." It was "illegal" to aid and comfort a Jew in Hitler's Germany. But I am sure that if I had lived in Germany during that time I would have aided and comforted my Jewish brothers even though it was illegal. If I lived in a Communist country today where certain principles dear to the Christian faith are suppressed, I believe I would openly advocate disobeying these anti-religious laws. I must make two honest confessions to you, my Christian and Jewish brothers. First, I must confess that over the last few years I have been gravely disappointed with the white moderate. I have almost reached the regrettable conclusion that the Negro's great stumbling block in the stride toward freedom is not the White Citizen's Counciler or the Ku Klux Klanner, but the white moderate who is more devoted to "order" than to justice; who prefers a negative peace which is the absence of tension to a positive peace which is the presence of justice; who constantly says "I agree with you in the goal you seek, but I can't agree with your methods of direct action"; who paternalistically feels that he can set the timetable for another man's freedom; who lives by the myth of time and who constantly advises the Negro to wait until a "more convenient season." Shallow understanding from people of goodwill is more frustrating than absolute misunderstanding from people of ill will. Lukewarm acceptance is much more bewildering than outright rejection.

I had hoped that the white moderate would understand that law and order exist for the purpose of establishing justice, and that when they fail to do this they become dangerously structured dams that block the flow of social progress. I had hoped that the white moderate would understand that the present tension in the South is merely a necessary phase of the transition from an obnoxious negative peace, where the Negro passively accepted his unjust plight, to a substance-filled positive peace, where all men will respect the dignity and worth of human personality. Actually, we who engage in nonviolent direct action are not the creators of tension. We merely bring to the surface the hidden tension that is already alive. We bring it out in the open where it can be seen and dealt with. Like a boil that can never be cured as long as it is covered up but must be opened with all its pus-flowing ugliness to the natural medicines of air and light, injustice must likewise be exposed, with all of the tension its exposing creates, to the light of human conscience and the air of national opinion before it can be cured.

In your statement you asserted that our actions, even though peaceful, must be condemned because they precipitate violence. But can this assertion be logically made? Isn't this like condemning the robbed man because his possession of money precipitated the evil act of robbery?

Never before have I written a letter this long (or should I say a book?). I'm afraid that it is much too long to take your precious time. I can assure you that it would have been much shorter if I had been writing from a comfortable desk, but what else is there to do when you are alone for days in the dull monotony of a narrow jail cell other than write long letters, think strange thoughts, and pray long prayers?

If I have said anything in this letter that is an over-statement of the truth and is indicative of an unreasonable impatience, I beg you to forgive me. If I have said anything in this letter that is an understatement of the truth and is indicative of my having a patience that makes me patient with anything less than brotherhood, I beg God to forgive me.

I hope this letter finds you strong in the faith. I also hope that circumstances will soon make it possible for me to meet each of you, not as an integrationist or a civil rights leader, but as a fellow clergyman and a Christian brother. Let us all hope that the dark clouds of racial prejudice will soon pass away and the deep fog of misunderstanding will be lifted from our fear-drenched communities and in some not too distant tomorrow the radiant stars of love and brotherhood will shine over our great nation with all of their scintillating beauty.

Yours for the cause of Peace and Brotherhood
Martin Luther King, Jr.

From Rev. King's address at the March on Washington, August, 1964:

I say to you today, my friends, though, even though we face the difficulties of today and tomorrow, I still have a dream. It is a dream deeply rooted in the American dream. I have a dream that one day this nation will rise up, live out the true meaning of its creed: "We hold these truths to be self-evident, that all men are created equal."

I have a dream that one day on the red hills of Georgia sons of former slaves and the sons of former slave-owners will be able to sit down together at the table of brotherhood. I have a dream that one day even the state of Mississippi, a state sweltering with the heat of injustice, sweltering with the heat of oppression, will be transformed into an oasis of freedom and justice.

I have a dream that my four little children will one day live in a nation where they will not be judged by the color of their skin but by the content of their character. I have a dream . . . I have a dream that one day in Alabama, with its vicious racists, with its governor having his lips dripping with the words of interposition and nullification, one day right there in Alabama little black boys and black girls will be able to join hands with little white boys and white girls as sisters and brothers.

I have a dream today . . . I have a dream that one day every valley shall be exalted, every hill and mountain shall be made low. The rough places will be made plain, and the crooked places will be made straight. And the glory of the Lord shall be revealed, and all flesh shall see it together. This is our hope. This is the faith that I go back to the South with. With this faith we will be able to hew out of the mountain of despair a stone of hope. With this faith we will be able to transform the jangling discords of our nation into a beautiful symphony of brotherhood. With this faith we will be able to work together, to pray together, to struggle together, to go to jail together, to stand up for freedom together, knowing that we will be free one day.

This will be the day when all of God's children will be able to sing with new meaning, "My country, 'tis of thee, sweet land of liberty, of thee I sing. Land where my fathers died, land of the pilgrim's pride, from every mountain side, let freedom ring." And if America is to be a great nation this must become true. So let freedom ring from the prodigious hilltops of New Hampshire. Let freedom ring from the mighty mountains of New York. Let freedom ring from the heightening Alleghenies of Pennsylvania. Let freedom ring from the snow-capped Rockies of Colorado. Let freedom ring from the curvaceous slopes of California.

But not only that. Let freedom ring from Stone Mountain of Georgia. Let freedom ring from Lookout Mountain of Tennessee. Let freedom ring from every hill and molehill of Mississippi, from every mountain side. Let freedom ring . . . .

When we allow freedom to ring—when we let it ring from every city and every hamlet, from every state and every city, we will be able to speed up that day when all of God's children, black men and white men, Jews and Gentiles, Protestants and Catholics, will be able to join hands and sing in the words of the old Negro spiritual, "Free at last, Free at last, Great God almighty, We are free at last."

White and Nonwhite Education and Employment*

THE GAP BETWEEN NONWHITE AND WHITE UNEMPLOYMENT RATES PERSISTS IN BOOM YEARS AS WELL AS RECESSION, BUT NARROWS SUBSTANTIALLY IN AN EXPANDING ECONOMY

LITTLE MORE THAN HALF OF ALL NONWHITE MALES WHO WORKED IN 1964 HAD FULL-TIME YEAR-ROUND JOBS, COMPARED WITH TWO-THIRDS OF ALL WHITE MALES

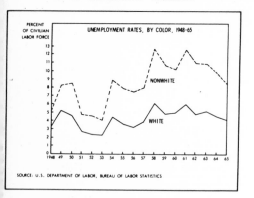

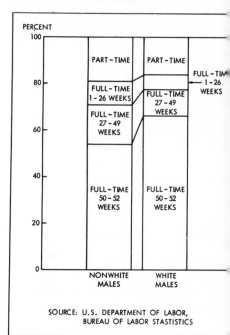

NEVERTHELESS, THE RATIO OF NONWHITE TO WHITE UNEMPLOYMENT RATES HAS REMAINED OVER 2.0 AND HAS BEEN CONSISTENTLY HIGHER FOR NONWHITE ADULT MEN THAN FOR OTHER NONWHITES

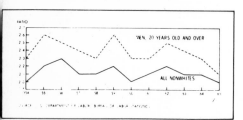

A LARGER PROPORTION OF NONWHITE THAN WHITE MALE HIGH SCHOOL GRADUATES* HOLD BLUE-COLLAR JOBS**

BUT A HIGH SCHOOL DIPLOMA IMPROVES THE NONWHITE WORKER'S CHANCES OF MOVING FROM LABORER TO PRODUCTION AND CRAFTS JOBS

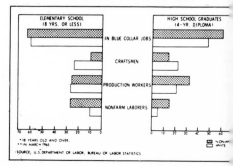

*Government charts from the U.S. Dept. of Labor, The Negroes in the U.S., Bulletin No. 1511, June, 1966, pp. 20-26.

SCHOOL ENROLLMENT RATES ARE ABOUT AS GREAT AMONG NONWHITE AS WHITE YOUTH 7-17, BUT ARE MUCH LESS FOR NONWHITES IN THE KINDERGARTEN AND COLLEGE YEARS

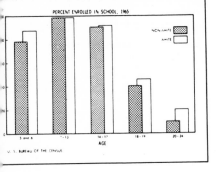

UNEMPLOYMENT RATES WERE HIGHER FOR NONWHITE HIGH-SCHOOL GRADUATES* THAN FOR WHITE DROPOUTS**
OCTOBER 1965

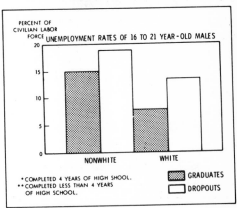

NONWHITE HIGH SCHOOL GRADUATES (AGED 16–21) ARE MUCH MORE LIKELY THAN THE WHITE TO HAVE PARENTS WHO ARE NOT HIGH SCHOOL GRADUATES AND TO COME FROM VERY LOW-INCOME FAMILIES

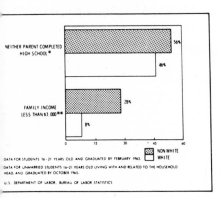

WEEKLY EARNINGS ON FULL-TIME JOBS WERE LOWER FOR NONWHITE GRADUATES THAN FOR WHITE DROPOUTS
FEBRUARY 1963

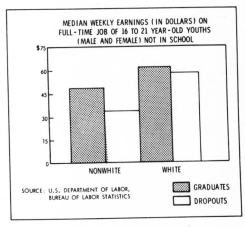

NONWHITE FAMILIES WERE ABOUT HALF AS LIKELY AS THE WHITE TO BE HOMEOWNERS
(1960)

White and Nonwhite Housing*

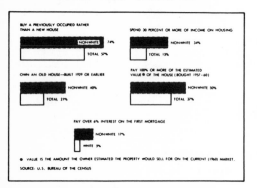

NONWHITE HOMEOWNERS WERE MORE LIKELY THAN OTHERS TO--

NONWHITE SUBSTANDARD HOUSING UNITS INCREASED GREATLY, IN PROPORTION TO ALL HOUSING UNITS, 1950 - 60, WHEREAS THE RELATIVE NUMBER OF NONWHITE HOUSEHOLDS SCARCELY CHANGED

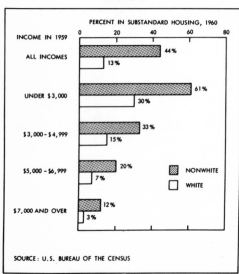

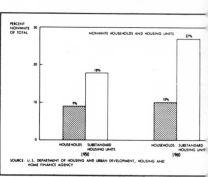

AT EVERY INCOME LEVEL RELATIVELY MORE NONWHITE THAN WHITE HOUSEHOLDS OCCUPIED SUBSTANDARD HOUSING

40 PERCENT OF ALL NONWHITE CHILDREN IN 1960 LIVED IN OVERCROWDED HOUSING OR HOUSING LACKING SOME FACILITIES*

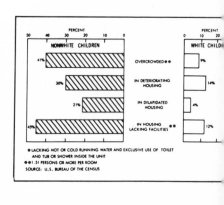

*Government charts from the U.S. Dept. of Labor, The Negroes in the U.S., Bulletin No. 1511, June, 1966, pp. 39-42

PERCENT OF NONWHITE MARRIED WOMEN WITH HUSBANDS ABSENT DUE TO SEPARATION AND OTHER REASONS, 1960

City	Percent with Husband Absent due to Separation and Other Reasons	Percent Separated
Akron	16.1	11.9
Birmingham	18.5	13.8
Mobile	23.5	16.4
Denver	14.2	9.5
Hartford	25.7	19.9
Wilmington	23.9	17.3
Washington	23.5	16.1
Chicago	23.5	18.7
Detroit	19.2	14.9
St. Louis	23.1	18.5
New York City	30.2	21.5
Buffalo	22.3	17.7
Philadelphia	25.3	19.5
Pittsburgh	19.7	15.1
Baltimore	23.0	16.6
Houston	15.3	11.4
Dallas	17.2	11.8
San Antonio	16.1	9.0
Cleveland	18.5	14.1
Cincinnati	20.6	15.7
Milwaukee	18.2	13.5
Boston	23.5	15.9
New Orleans	22.2	15.7
Seattle	13.8	8.7
Memphis	22.6	17.7
Atlanta	22.6	16.8

Source: *U.S. Census of Population*, Vol. 1 –Selected States, table 105.

PERCENT OF WHITE AND NONWHITE CHILDREN UNDER 18 NOT LIVING WITH BOTH PARENTS, UNITED STATES, URBAN AND RURAL, 1960

Area	Children Under 18 Without Both Parents	
	White	Nonwhite
United States	10.0	33.7
Urban.............................	10.3	35.1
Rural Nonfarm	10.1	32.7
Rural Farm..........................	6.6	26.5

e U.S. Dept. of
The Negro Family,
1965, pp. 57-62.

Source: *U.S. Census of Population, 1960, Social and Economic Characteristics* PC (1)-1(C), table 79, p. 210.

Excerpts from the Official Summary
of the Report of the President's
National Advisory Commission on Civil Disorders

February, 1968

The Conclusion

Our nation is moving toward two societies, one black, one white—separate and unequal. Reaction to last summer's disorders has quickened the movement and deepened the division. Discrimination and segregation have long permeated much of American life; they now threaten the future of every American. This deepening racial division is not inevitable. The movement apart can be reversed. Choice is still possible. Our principal task is to define that choice and to press for a national resolution . . . .

Riot Patterns

In general: The civil disorders of 1967 involved Negroes acting against local symbols of white American society, authority and property in Negro neighborhoods—rather than against white persons.

    —Of 164 disorders reported during the first nine months of 1967, eight (5 percent) were major in terms of violence and damage; 33 (20 percent) were serious but not major; 123 (75 percent) were minor and undoubtedly would not have received national attention as "riots" had the nation not been sensitized by the more serious outbreaks.

    —In the 75 disorders studied by a Senate subcommittee, there were 83 deaths. Eighty-two percent of the deaths and more than half the injuries occurred in Newark and Detroit. About 10 percent of the dead and 36 percent of the injured were public employees, primarily law officers and firemen. The overwhelming majority of the persons killed or injured in all the disorders were Negro civilians.

—Initial damage estimates were greatly exaggerated. In Detroit, newspaper damage estimates at first ranged from $200 million to $500 million; the highest recent estimate is $45 million. In Newark, early estimates ranged from $15 million to $25 million. A month later damage was estimated at $10.2 million, 80 percent in inventory losses.

Who were the rioters? The typical rioter was a teenager or young adult, a life-long resident of the city in which he rioted, a high school dropout; he was, nevertheless, somewhat better educated than his nonrioting Negro neighbor, and was usually underemployed or employed in a menial job. He was proud of his race, extremely hostile to both whites and middleclass Negroes and, although informed about politics, highly distrustful of the political system.

—In a survey of Negro males between the ages of 15 and 35 residing in the disturbance area in Newark, about 45 percent identified themselves as rioters, and about 55 percent as "noninvolved." But a Detroit survey revealed that only approximately 11 percent of the total residents of two riot areas participated in the rioting, over 16 percent identified themselves as "counter-rioters" who urged rioters to "cool it," and about 73 percent identified themselves as "noninvolved."

—Most rioters were young Negro males. Nearly 53 percent of the arrestees were between 15 and 24 years of age; nearly 81 percent between 15 and 35.

—In Detroit and Newark about 74 percent of the rioters were brought up in the North. In contrast, of the noninvolved, 36 percent in Detroit and 52 percent in Newark were brought up in the North.

Basic Causes

White Racism
White racism is essentially responsible for the explosive mixture which has been accumulating in our cities since the end of World War II. At the base of this mixture are three of the most bitter fruits of white racial attitudes:
   —Pervasive discrimination and segregation in employ-

ment, education, and housing have resulted in the continuing exclusion of great numbers of Negroes from the benefits of economic progress.

—Black in-migration and white exodus have produced the massive and growing concentrations of impoverished Negroes in our major cities, creating a growing crisis of deteriorating facilities and services and unmet human needs.

—In the black ghettos segregation and poverty converge on the young to destroy opportunity and enforce failure. Crime, drug addiction, dependency on welfare, and bitterness and resentment against society in general and white society in particular are the result.

These three forces have converged on the inner city in recent years and on the people who inhabit it. At the same time, most whites and many Negroes outside the ghetto have prospered to a degree unparalleled in the history of civilization. Through television and other media, this affluence has been endlessly flaunted before the eyes of the Negro poor and the jobless ghetto youth.

Other Ingredients

Yet these facts alone cannot be said to have caused the disorders. Recently, other powerful ingredients have begun to catalyze the mixture:

—Frustrated hopes are the residue of the unfulfilled expectations aroused by the great judicial and legislative victories of the Civil Rights movement and the dramatic struggle for equal rights in the South.

—A climate that tends toward approval and encouragement of violence as a form of protest has been created by white terrorism directed against nonviolent protest; by the open defiance of law and federal authority by state and local officials resisting desegregation; and by some protest groups engaging in civil disobedience who turn their backs on nonviolence, go beyond the constitutionally protected rights of petition and free assembly, and resort to violence to attempt to compel alteration of laws and policies with which they disagree.

—The frustrations of powerlessness have led some Negroes to the conviction that there is no effective alternative to violence as a means of achieving redress of grievances, and of "moving the system." These frustrations are reflected in alienation and hostility toward the institutions of law and government and the white society which controls them, and in the reach toward racial consciousness and solidarity reflected in the slogan "Black Power."

Recommendations

Job Programs

The Commission recommends that the federal government:

—Undertake joint efforts with cities and states to consolidate existing manpower programs to avoid fragmentation and duplication.

—Take immediate action to create two million new jobs over the next three years—one million in the public sector and one million in the private sector.

—To absorb the hard-core unemployed and materially reduce the level of underemployment for all workers black and white. We propose 250,000 public sector and 300,000 private sector jobs in the first year.

—Provide on-the-job training by both public and private employers with reimbursement to private employers for the extra costs of training the hard-core unemployed, by contract or by tax credits.

School Proposals

The Commission recommends:

—Sharply increased efforts to eliminate de facto segregation in our schools through substantial federal aid to school systems seeking to desegregate either within the system or in cooperation with neighboring school systems.

—Elimination of racial discrimination in northern as well as southern schools by vigorous application of Title

VI of the Civil Rights Act of 1964.

—Expanding the quality of early childhood education to every disadvantaged child in the country.

—Efforts to improve dramatically schools serving disadvantaged children through substantial federal funding of year-round quality compensatory education programs, improved teaching, and expanded experimentation and research.

—Elimination of illiteracy through greater federal support for adult basic education.

—Enlarged opportunities for parent and community participation in the public schools.

—Reoriented vocational education emphasizing work-experience training and the involvement of business and industry.

—Expanded opportunities for higher education through increased federal assistance to disadvantaged students.

—Revision of state aid formulas to assure more per student aid to districts having a high proportion of disadvantaged school-age children.

Other Recommendations

—Establish uniform national standards of assistance at least as high as the annual "poverty level" of income, now set by the Social Security Administration at $3,335 for an urban family of four.

—Require that all states receiving federal welfare contributions participate in the Aid to Families with Dependent Children-Unemployed Parents program (AFDC-UP) that permits assistance to families with both father and mother in the home, thus aiding the family while it is still intact.

—Federal government bear a substantially greater portion of all welfare costs—at least 90 percent of total payment.

—Increase incentives for seeking employment and job training, but remove restrictions recently enacted by the Congress that would compel mothers of young children to work.

—Bring within the reach of low and moderate income families within the next five years, six million new and existing units of decent housing, beginning with 600,000 units in the next year.

The Time is Now

We have provided an honest beginning. We have learned much. But we have uncovered no startling truths, no unique insights, no simple solutions. The destruction and bitterness of racial disorder, the harsh polemics of black revolt and white repression have been seen and heard before in this country.

It is time now to end the destruction and the violence, not only in the streets of the ghetto but in the lives of people.

Bibliography

Rather than attempt to provide a complete listing of the scores of important volumes in the field of race relations, the author will confine himself to recommending a few books that he has found most helpful in the preparation of this text and that he would bring to the attention of the interested reader.

1.) Silberman, Charles E. *Crisis in Black and White.* New York, Random House, 1964. A superb blend of scholarship, moral commitment and readability. In this author's opinion, the best single volume on the "Negro Revolt" for the general reader.

2.) Clark, Kenneth. *Dark Ghetto.* New York, Harper and Row, 1965. A sober scholarly and penetrating look behind the invisible walls of the Negro ghetto by a noted psychologist.

3.) Lomax, Louis E. *The Negro Revolt.* New York, Harper and Row, 1962. Valuable particularly for its clear coverage of the early background of the revolt and for its discussion of the organizational and ideological splits within the Negro community in the early 1960's.

4.) Marx, Gary. *Protest and Prejudice: A Study of Belief in the Black Community.* New York, Harper and Row, 1967. An empirical study of the Negro community that challenges impressions received through the mass media and that includes a careful analysis of Negro anti-Semitism.

5.) Baldwin, James. *Notes of a Native Son.* Boston Beacon Press, 1955. Of all Baldwin's works, this first collection of autobiographical essays may be his most sensitive writing on the theme of being a Negro in America. Read especially the essay, "Notes of a Native Son."

6.) Brown, Claude. *Manchild in the Promised Land.* New York, Macmillan, 1965. A vivid picture of life in Harlem "the way it is" written with candor but without self-pity by one who somehow managed to "make it."

7.) Gordis, Robert. *The Root and the Branch: Judaism and the Free Society.* Chicago, University of Chicago Press, 1962. A fine demonstration of the relevance of Jewish tradition to the moral issues of our time. See chapters on "race and the religious tradition" and "ethics and the political process."

8.) Rackman, Emanuel. *Jewish Values for Modern Man.* New York, Jewish Education Committee, 1962. A scholarly exploration of Jewish law that seeks out the traditional view on current issues.

9.) Hirsch, Richard. *There Shall Be No Poor.* New York, Union of American Hebrew Congregations, 1965. A clear presentation of the problem of poverty, motivated by Judaism's traditional concern with economic justice.

10.) *American Jewish Year Book*, 1955 to the present. In each year book there is a section on civil rights, by Lucy Dawidowicz, Theodore Leskes or Harry Fleischman. This excellent summary is probably the best chronological history of the Civil Rights movement available.

11.) Vorspan, Albert. *Jewish Values and Social Crisis: A Casebook for Social Action.* New York, Union of American Hebrew Congregations, 1968. This high school text aims to stimulate personal involvement and class discussion through sociodramas that confront the student with the necessity of making a choice and taking a stand. The chapters on race relations and poverty may well be used in conjunction with *Justice, Justice.*

12.) Lipman, Eugene and Vorspan, Albert. *Justice and Judaism.* New York, Union of American Hebrew Congregations, 1956. This was the first book written for teen-agers (as well as adults) that systematically viewed social problems in the light of Jewish ideals.

13.) Report of the National Advisory Commission on Civil Disorders, a Bantam Book, March, 1968. The now classic study of the what, how, and why of urban riots, conducted by the Kerner Commission and readily available in this paperback edition. Compare Chapter Nine with the section in Chapter Four of *Justice, Justice,* on why blacks are having even greater difficulty than other groups had in becoming part of the American mainstream.

Because of the current interest in the implications of black self-determination for the Jewish and general community, the following books and articles are listed according to subject matter:

ON BLACK SELF-DETERMINATION AND JEWISH NATIONALISM

Bennet, Lerone. *The Negro Mood.* New York, Ballantine Books, 1964.

Borochov, Ber. *Nationalism and the Class Struggle.* New York, Poale Zion, 1937.

Carmichael, Stokely and Hamilton, Charles V. *Black Power: The Politics of Liberation in America.* New York, Vintage 1967.

Cleaver, Eldridge. *Soul on Ice.* New York, McGraw Hill, 1968.

Cleaver, Eldridge. *Post Prison Writings and Speeches.* New York, Random House, a Ramparts Book, 1969.

Cruse, Harold. *The Crisis of the Negro Intellectual.* New York, William Morrow & Co., Apollo Edition, 1967.

Dubnow, Simon M. *History of the Jews in Russia and Poland.* 3 volumes. Philadelphia, Jewish Publication Society, 1946.

Hertzberg, Arthur. *The Zionist Idea.* Garden City, New York, Doubleday and Herzl Press, 1959.

Malcolm X. *The Autobiography of Malcolm X.* New York, Grove, 1964.

Patkin, A.L. *The Origins of the Russian-Jewish Labor Movement.* London, Cheshire, 1947.

Sachar, Howard. *The Course of Modern Jewish History.* New York, World (Dell Ed.) 1958.

Saperstein, Marc. "Nationalism and the Dilemma of the American Jewish Liberal." *Dimensions,* Vol. III, No. 3, Spring, 1969.

ON COMMUNITY CONTROL OF SCHOOLS

Cohen, David K. "The Price of Community Control." *Commentary,* July, 1969, Vol. 48:1, pp. 23-32.

American Society for Public Administration. "A Symposium: Alienation, Decentralization, and Participation." *Public Administration Review,* January-February, 1969, pp. 2-63.

DeLone, Richard H. "A Tale of Three Cities: Decentralization and Community Control." The School District of Philadelphia.

Epstein, Jason. "The Issue at Ocean Hill." *The New York Review of Books*, Vol. XI, No. 2, Nov. 21, 1968, pp. 3 ff. (and 2 subsequent issues).

Fantini, M.D. "Alternatives for Urban School Reform." *Harvard Educational Review*, Vol. 38, No. 1, Winter, 1968.

Feldman, Sandra. "Decentralization and the City Schools." *Looking Forward*, No. 12 in a Series of Occasional Papers, League for Industrial Democracy, New York, New York.

Finney, Graham. "Recent History of Administrative Decentralization" and "Community Participation in the Schools of Philadelphia." The School District of Philadelphia.

Goldbloom, Maurice J. "The New York School Crisis." *Commentary*, Jan. 1969, Vol. 47:1, pp. 43-58.

Haskins, Kenneth W. "The Case for Local Control." *Saturday Review*, Jan. 11, 1969, pp. 52-54.

Mayer, Martin. "The Full and Surprising Story of Ocean Hill." *New York Times Magazine*, Feb. 2, 1969, pp. 18-23ff.

New York Civil Liberties Union. *The Burden of Blame*. A Report on the Ocean Hill-Brownsville School Controversy, (Pamphlet) 156 Fifth Ave., New York, N.Y. 10010, Oct. 1968.

Rogers, David. *110 Livingston Street*. Random House, N.Y. City, 1968.

Stone, I.F. "The Mason Dixon Line Moves to New York." *I.F. Stone's Weekly*, Nov. 4, 1968, Washington, D.C., Vol. XVL, No. 22.

A NEW LOOK AT BLACK ANTI-SEMITISM

"Anti-Semitism in New York City Schools." *The Metropolitan Star*, Anti-Defamation League of B'nai B'rith. New York, Jan. 1969.

Friedman, Murray. "Is White Racism the Problem?" *Commentary*, Jan. 1969, Vol. 47:1, pp. 61-5.

Gans, Herbert. "Negro-Jewish Conflict in New York City." *Midstream*, March, 1969, pp. 3-15.

Glazer, Nathan. "Blacks, Jews and Intellectuals." *Commentary*, April, 1969, Vol. 47:4, pp. 33-9.

Hatchett, John H. "The Phenomenon of the Anti-Black Jews and the Black Anglo-Saxons." *African-American Teachers Forum*, Nov., 1967.

Lindeman, Yehudi. Urban Crisis and Jewish Law. *Hadassah Magazine* March, 1969, pp. 10 ff.

Marx, Gary. *Protest and Prejudice: A Study of Belief in the Black Community.* New York, Harper and Row, 1967.

Marx, Robert. "The People in Between." *Dimensions in American Judaism*, Vol. III, No. 3, Spring, 1969. UAHC.

Raab, Earl. "The Black Revolution and the Jewish Question." *Commentary*, Jan., 1969, Vol. 47:1, pp. 61-5.

NOTES

Chapter One: A Way of Viewing

1. *Amos* 5:11-15.

2. *Zeraim: Peah,* 2.

3. *Isaiah* 49:6.

4. As quoted by Newman, *Talmudic Anthology,* p. 234. cf. *Sanhedrin,* 32b, *Tanhuma,* Buber to *Shofetim* 5 and 7.

5. M. Buber, *Ten Rungs,* p. 81.

6. Quoted by E. Raab, *American Race Relations Today,* pp. 14-15.

7. *Mishnah Avot* 2:6.

8. I. Newman, *Hasidic Anthology,* p. 221.

9. J. H. Griffin, *Black Like Me.*

10. *Leviticus* 19:18.

11. R. Gordis, *The Root and the Branch,* p. 156.

12. *Matthew* 5:39-40.

13. *Mishnah Avot* 5:13.

14. P. Tillich, *Love, Power, and Justice,* p. 57: "If life as the actuality of being is essentially the drive towards the reunion of the separated, it follows that the justice of being is the form which is adequate to this movement."

15. *Mishnah Avot* 2:30.

16. *Taanit* 112, from L. Browne, *Wisdom of Israel,* p. 197.

Chapter Two: How Do You Answer a Revolution?

1. L. Lomax, *The Negro Revolt,* pp. 81-100.

2. M. Buber (ed.), *Tales of the Hasidim,* Vol. 2, p. 315.

3. M. L. King, *Why We Can't Wait,* p. 113.

4. C. Silberman, *Crisis in Black and White,* p. 143.

5. Mishneh Torah, Hilkot Melakim, III, 9 quoted in E. Rackman. *Jewish Values for Modern Man,* JEC Press, p. 26.

6. E. Rackman, *op. cit.,* p. 27.

7. A. Vorspan, "In St. Augustine," *Midstream,* September, 1964.

8.   "Why We Went," Social Action Commission, UAHC.

9.   L. S. Dawidowicz, "Civil Rights and Intergroup Tensions," *American Jewish Year Book,* 1965, p. 185.

10. Report by Asa D. Sokolow on Mississippi, *Judaism in Social Action* (United Synagogue of America), January, 1965, pp. 10-13. This reference as well as much of the data on the Civil Rights movement may be found in the excellent annual review of "Civil Rights and Intergroup Tensions," by Lucy S. Dawidowicz, in the *American Jewish YearBooks,* 1955 to present. This report was received with skepticism by some who observed the events of that summer.

11. B. Rustin, "From Protest to Politics," *Commentary,* February, 1965, pp. 25-27.

12. Statistics taken from *The Negroes in the U.S.,* Bulletin No. 1511, U.S. Dept. of Labor, June, 1966.

13. *Ibid.*

14. *Manpower Report of the President,* Table A-13, by the U.S. Dept. of Labor, March, 1966.

15. A. Rosen, introduction to Berson's "Case Study of a Riot," *Institute of Human Relations Press,* p. 9.

16. For description and discussion of Alinsky's technique, see Silberman, *Crisis in Black and White,* pp. 317-355.

17. J. Conant, *Slums and Suburbs.*

18. H. Fleishman, "Civil Rights," *American Jewish Year Book,* 1966, p. 120.

19. *New York Times,* July 12, 1969.

20. M. Harrington, "The Other America Revisited," *The Center Magazine,* vol. II:1, Jan., 1969, pp. 36-41.

21. NBC News, July 27, 1967.

22. G. Marx, *Protest and Prejudice: A Study of Belief in the Black Community,* pp. 25, 30, 32, 108-9.

23. *New York Times,* July 7, 1968.

24. *U.S. News and World Report,* Feb. 17, 1969, pp. 60 ff.

25. E. Raab, "The Black Revolution and the Jewish Question," *Commentary,* vol. 47:1, pp. 28-9.

26. M. Lerner, *ADL. Bulletin,* June, 1968, p. 4.

27. S. Carmichael and C. Hamilton, *Black Power: The Politics of Liberation in America,* pp. 58-81.

28. L. Lomax, *op. cit.*, pp. 185, 198.

29. G. Myrdal, *The American Dilemma.*

Chapter Three: What Do You Really Believe About Equality?

1. This interpretation of human equality is based on H.A. Myers, *Are Men Equal?*

2. H. S. Broudy, "What Can the School Say about Human Rights?" *Phi Delta Kappa*, May, 1966, p. 467.

3. M. Cranston, *What Are Human Rights?*

4. Myers, *op. cit.*, p. 177.

5. S. Hook, "Naturalism and Democracy," from Y. Krikorian, *Naturalism and the Human Spirit*, p. 49.

6. R. Kirk, *The Conservative Mind*, p. 82.

7. R. Kirk, *Program for Conservatives*, pp. 169-170.

8. *Mishnah Avot* 3:18.

9. Quoted in H. Cohen, "The Idea of God in Jewish Education," *Judaism*, Vol. 12, No. 2, Spring, 1963, p. 172.

10. R. Gordis, *op. cit.*, pp. 158-159.

11. *Leviticus* 24:22. See also *Numbers* 15:14.

12. *Leviticus* 19:10 and 23:22.

13. J. Randall, *The Making of the Modern Mind*, pp. 313-318.

14. M. Kaplan, *The Meaning of God in Modern Jewish Religion*, p. 53.

15. A. H. Maslow, *Motivation and Personality*, p. 217.

16. M. Buber, *Between Man and Man*, p. 110.

17. M. Kaplan, *The Purpose and Meaning of Jewish Existence*, p. 295.

18. *Exodus* 23:9 (JPS New Translation) "You know the feelings of the stranger."

19. C. Silberman, *op. cit.*, pp. 74-77.

20. This section is a condensed version of H. Cohen, "How Big is the Jewish Backlash," *National Jewish Monthly*, January, 1965, p. 6.

21. G. Allport, *The Nature of Prejudice*, p. 155.

22. *Deuteronomy* 23:15-16. See discussion of slavery in Jewish law by R. Gordis, *The Root and the Branch*, pp. 118-120, and G. Horowitz *op. cit.*, pp. 244-252.

23. *Exodus* 21:2.

24. *Baba Kama* 113b, as interpreted in G. Horowitz, *The Spirit of Jewish Law*, p. 235.

25. G. Horowitz, *op. cit.*, pp. 235-236.

26. *Gittin* 61a.

27. *Tosefta N'gaim*, 86; *Talmud Yerushalmi: Yebamot* 88a, as quoted in *Encyclopedia Talmudit*, Vol. 6, pp. 291-294.

28. Katz, *Exclusiveness and Tolerance*, pp. 30-31, 60.

29. Katz, *op. cit.*, p. 101.

30. G. Horowitz, *op. cit.*, p. 237 (Quoting *Mishnah Torah*, XVIII, 1).

31. Quoted in Responses by I. J. Unterman, excerpt in *Tradition*, Vol. 8, No. 2, Summer, 1966.

32. G. Horowitz, *op. cit.*, p. 238. (Quoting: Landau, *Resp.* Intro.)

33. *Mishnah Avot* 2:17..

34. G. Horowitz, *op. cit.*, p. 123, Law based on *Deuteronomy* 22:8.

35. *Hoshen Mishpat*, p. 427, and Nizzekuni cited by G. Horowitz, *ibid.*

36. Cited by R. Hirsch, *There Shall Be No Poor*, p. 12.

37. J. Peck, *Freedom Ride*, pp. 28-29.

Chapter Four: The Question of Responsibility

1. *Yalkut Shim'oni (Yalkut)* I: 13, as translated in Simon and Bial's *The Rabbis Bible*, p. 11. See also *Sanhedrin* 4:5.

2. A. Montagu, *Statement on Race*, p. 87.

3. A. Montagu, *What We Know About Race*, Anti-Defamation League pamphlet, pp. 26-30.

4. A. Montagu, *Statement on Race*, p. 102.

5. M. E. Wolfgang, *Crime and Race*, p. 34.

6. C. Putnam, *Race and Reason*.

7. C. Silberman, *op. cit.*, pp. 258-261.

8. A. Montagu, *Statement on Race*, p. 90.

9. *Genesis* 9:25-27. See discussion in Gordis, *op. cit.*, p. 121.

10. J. Conant, *Slums* and *Suburbs*, pp. 19-30.

11. B. Rustin, *op. cit.*, p. 26.

12. The President's *Manpower Report to Congress*, 1965, quoted in "New America" July 25, 1965, p. 3. See debate on this question between Charles Silberman and Michael Harrington.

13. R. Heilbroner, "Automation in the Perspective of Long-Term Technological Change," U.S. Dept. of Labor, December 1966, p. 14.

14. B. Rustin, *ibid.*

15. "The Negro Family," U.S. Dept. of Labor, March, 1965, p. 9.

16. C. Silberman, *op. cit.,* p. 115.

17. *Ibid,* p. 41.

18. H. Fleishman, *op. cit.,* p. 114.

19. *The Negroes in the U.S., op. cit.,* p. 24.

20. C. Brown, *Manchild in the Promised Land,* p. 280.

21. J. Conant, *op. cit.,* p. 10.

22. K. Clark, *Dark Ghetto,* pp. 132-137.

23. Quoted by Silberman, *op. cit.,* p. 10.

24. L. Berson, *op. cit.,* pp. 32-39.

25. K. Clark, *Dark Ghetto,* p. 30.

26. S. Lubell, *White and Black,* p. 148.

27. K. Clark, *op. cit.,* p. 1.

28. *Ibid,* p. 2.

29. C. Brown, *op. cit.,* p. 122.

30. J. Baldwin, *The Fire Next Time.*

31. Quoted in Silberman, *op. cit.,* p. 36.

32. M. E. Wolfgang, *Crime and Race,* p. 56.

33. L. Lomax, *op. cit.,* pp. 216-217.

34. *The New York Times Magazine,* September 5, 1965.

35. A. Rosen, *op. cit.,* p. 6.

36. L. Berson, *op. cit.,* pp. 50-53.

37. *The Challenge of Crime in a Free Society,* Report of the President's Commission on Law Enforcement and Administration of Justice, February, 1967, p. 37.

38. *New York Times,* July 28, 1968.

39. *Philadelphia Evening Bulletin,* August 8, 1967.

40. *Mishnah Avot 2:5*

Chapter Five: Into the Mainstream

1. R. Sackett, "Plotting a War on Whitey," *Life,* June 10, 1966, p. 106.

2. C. Silberman, *op. cit.,* pp. 238-241.

3. L. Lomax, *op. cit.*, p. 213.

4. A "Freedom Budget" for All Americans, (A summary), A. Philip Randolph Institute, January, 1967, p. 19.

5. From Rev. King's remarks on the Merv Griffin Show, July 6, 1967.

6. A "Freedom Budget" for All Americans, pp. 42-55. (A. Philip Randolph Institute), October, 1966.

7. R. Hirsch, *There Shall Be No Poor*, UAHC, pp. 9-27.

8. *Mishnah Peah* 8:7-8. See E. Frisch, *An Historical Survey of Jewish Philanthropy*, pp. 48-60. See also H. Danby, *The Mishna*, p. 20.

9. Hirsch, *op. cit.*, p. 24.

10. *Sifra* 109b, quoted by Hirsch, *op. cit.*, p. 22.

11. Maimonides, "Code of Benevolence," translation from *Union Prayer Book II*, p. 118.

12. *B. Makkot*, 10a.

13. E. Rackman, *op. cit.*, pp. 27-28.

14. *Tikkune Zohar*, 122, T. 43, quoted in Newman's *Talmudic Anthology*, p. 60.

15. M. Smilansky, "Fighting Deprivation in the Promised Land," *Saturday Review*, October 15, 1966, p. 185.

16. W. Young, newspaper column, Summer, 1965.

17. "The Myths of Racial Integration," American Jewish Congress.

18. M. E. Wolfgang, *op. cit.*, pp. 37-44. See also *The Challenge of Crime in a Free Society*, p. 40.

19. A. Montagu, *Statement on Race*, p. 108.

20. K. Clark, *op. cit.*, p. 230.

21. "Racial Intermarriage" (*Social Progress* reprint), February, 1960. p. 34.

22. H. Golden, *A Little Girl is Dead*, pp. 116-117. J. H. Griffin, *Black Like Me*, pp. 87-90.

23. M. Grodzins, "The Metropolitan Area as a Racial Problem," E. Raab (ed.) *American Race Relations Today*, p. 106.

24. *Main Line Times*, December 16, 1965.

25. Katz, *op. cit.*, p. 27. See *B.T., A.Z.*, 8a, 29b, 34a, and *Mishnah, A.Z.*, 1.6.

26. Katz, *op. cit.*, p. 41. See *Tosafoth* A.Z., 31b.

27. *Sifre* to *Deuteronomy* 23:17, *Tosephta N'gaim*, 86, quoted in Encyclopedia *Talmudit*, Vol. 6, pp. 291-294.

28. A. Schochat, "German Jews Integration," *Zion*, 1956, Vols. 3-4, pp. 207-235.

29. *Yalkut Shimoni*, see Chapter Four, note 1.

30. M. Buber, *Ten Rungs*, pp. 79-80.

31. *Brown vs. Board of Education*, 347 U.S. 483 (1954).

32. K. Clark, *op. cit.*, pp. 112-113.

33. C. Silberman, *op. cit.*, p. 304.

34. *Daedalus*, Winter, 1965, p. 281.

35. Haryou Report: *Youth in the Ghetto*, quoted in Silberman, *op. cit.*, pp. 306-307.

36. *Racial Isolation in the Public Schools*, U.S. Commission on Civil Rights, 1967, VI, p. 89.

37. Quoted in Silberman, *op. cit.*, p. 301.

38. *Ibid*, Summary, p. 4.

39. *Ibid*, Vol. 1, p. 104.

40. *Ibid*, Vol. 1, p. 91.

41. *Ibid*, Vol. 1, p. 160.

42. *Ibid*, Vol. 2, pp. 134-135.

43. *Shabbat* 119b.

44. "The Dialogue," NCCJ, June, 1963, p. 3.

45. L. Browne, *The Wisdom of Israel*, pp. 306-313.

Chapter Six: Black Self-determination and Jewish Nationalism

1. H. Cruse, *The Crisis of the Negro Intellectual*.

2. S. Carmichael and C. Hamilton, *Black Power: The Politics of Liberation in America*, p. 179.

3. E. Cleaver, *Post-Prison Writings and Speeches*, p. 67.

4. H. Cruse, *op. cit.*, p. 547.

5. E. Cleaver, *op. cit.*, p. 145.

6. R. Browne and B. Rustin, *Separatism or Integration: Which Way for America?* p. 15.

7. E. Cleaver, *op. cit.*, p. 66.

8. S. Carmichael and C. Hamilton, *op. cit.*, pp. 58-84.

9. E. Cleaver, *op. cit.*, p. 142.

10. R. Browne, *op. cit.*, p. 17.

11. L. Bennet, *The Negro Mood*, p. 89.

12. *The Autobiography of Malcolm X*, pp. 169-172.

13. O. Davis, "On Malcolm X," *op. cit.*, p. 458.

14. E. Raab, "The Black Revolution and the Jewish Question," *Commentary*, Jan., 1969, pp. 28-9.

15. *Mishnah Avot:* I:14.

16. R. Browne and B. Rustin, *op. cit.*, pp. 16-21.

17. H. Cruse, *op. cit.*, pp. 147-170.

18. E. Cleaver, *op. cit.*, p. 69

19. L. Pinsker, "Auto-emancipation," in A. Hertzberg (ed.), *The Zionist Idea*, pp. 194-8.

20. H. Sachar, *The Course of Modern Jewish History*, p. 291.

21. E. Cleaver, *op. cit.*, pp. 57-72.

22. I. Elbogen, *A Century of Jewish Life*, p. 390.

23. H. Sachar, *op. cit.*, p. 292.

24. B. Borochov, "Our Platform" in A. Hertzberg (ed) *op. cit.*, pp. 362-3.

25. L. Pinsker, *op. cit.*, p. 190.

26. A.D. Gordon, "Our Tasks Ahead," A Hertzberg (ed), *op. cit.*, p. 380.

27. L. Bennet, *op. cit.*, p. 115.

28. E. Cleaver, *op. cit.*, p. 66.

29. E. Rivkin, "The Age of Permanent Revolution," *Dimensions*, Winter, 1968-9.

30. E. Cleaver, *op. cit.*, pp. 71-2.

31. R. Browne and B. Rustin, *op. cit.*, p. 20.

Chapter Seven: Community Control and the Right to Power

1. Whitney Young, *Philadelphia Bulletin*, November 17, 1968.

2. G. Finney, "Recent History of Administrative Decentralization," The School District of Philadelphia, p. 1.

3. G. Finney, "Community Participation in the Schools of Philadelphia," The School District of Philadelphia, p. 1.

4. P. Goodman, "Letters to the Editor," *New York Times Magazine*, February 23, 1968.

5. R.H. DeLone, "A Tale of Three Cities: Decentralization and Community Control," The School District of Philadelphia, p. 76.

6. M.D. Fantini, "Alternatives for Urban School Reform," *Harvard Educational Review*, Vol. 38, No. 1, Winter, 1968.

7. *I.F. Stone's Weekly*, Vol. XVI, No. 22, November 24, 1968, p. 2.

8. D. Rogers, *110 Livingston Street*. pp. 288-9.

9. H. Cohen, *Justice, Justice*, pp. 106-7.

10. S. Carmichael and C. Hamilton, *op. cit.*, p. 167.

11. "Anti-Semitism in N.Y.C. Schools," *The Metropolitan Star*, Anti-Defamation League, N.Y., Jan., 1969, p. 10.

12. H. Mayer, "The Full and Surprising Story of Ocean Hill," *New York Times Magazine*, Feb. 2, 1968.

13. J.F. Hatchett, "The Phenomenon of the Anti-Black Jews and the Black Anglo-Saxon," *African-American Teachers Forum*, Nov., 1967, pp. 67 ff.

14. M. Goldbloom, "The New York School Crisis," *Commentary*, Jan., 1969, p. 58.

15. E. Cleaver, *op. cit.*, pp. 139-40.

16. *Ibid.*, p. 144.

17. Buber, M. (ed.) *Ten Rungs*, p. 7.

Chapter Eight: A New Look at Black Anti-Semitism

1. E. Raab, *op. cit.*, pp. 25-31.

2. G. Allport, *The Nature of Prejudice*, p. 19.

3. "Anti-Semitism in N.Y.C. Schools," *The Metropolitan Star*, Anti-Defamation League, New York, Jan. 1969, p. 10.

4. J.F. Hatchett, *op. cit.*

5. "Anti-Semitism in N.Y.C. Schools," p. 11.

6. N. Glazer, "Blacks, Jews and the Intellectuals," *Commentary*, April, 1969, p. 35.

7. D. Rogers, *op. cit.*, pp. 288-9.

8. H. Schulweis, "The Voice of Esau," *Reconstructionist,* Dec. 10, 1965., pp. 7-8, based on D. Caplovitz, *The Poor Pay More.*

9. L. Berson, *op. cit.,* p. 45.

10. H. Cruse, *op. cit.,* p. 167.

11. B. Rustin, *op. cit.,* p. 19.

12. *The Autobiography of Malcolm X, p. 372.*

13. G. Marx, *Protest and Prejudice,* pp. 126-7, 138.

14. N. Glazer, *op. cit.,* p. 33.

15. R. Gordis, "Negroes Are Anti-Semitic Because They Want a Scapegoat," *N.Y. Times Magazine,* April 16, 1967, p. 132.

16. J. Baldwin, *Notes of a Native Son,* pp. 66-7.

17. J. Baldwin, "Negroes Are Anti-Semitic Because They Are Anti-White," *N.Y. Times Magazine,* April 2, 1967, pp. 26, 136, 139.

18. Reported by B. Rustin, *Congress Bi-weekly,* May 23, 1966, p. 12.

19. J. Baldwin, *Notes of a Native Son,* p. 72.

20. J. Baldwin, "Negroes Are Anti-Semitic Because They Are Anti-White," pp. 136, 139.

21. R. Marx, "The People in Between," *Dimensions,* Vol. III, No. 3, pp. 8-10.

22. E. Raab, *op. cit.,* p. 30.

23. N. Glazer, *op. cit.,* p. 34.

24. *Ibid.,* p. 36.

25. H. Gans, "Negro-Jewish Conflict in New York City," *Midstream,* March, 1969, p. 3.

26. *Ibid.,* p. 8.

27. N. Glazer, *op. cit.,* p. 34.

28. For the story in Boston, see: Y. Lindeman, "Urban Crisis and Jewish Law," *Hadassah Magazine,* March, 1969. See also R. Marx, *op. cit.*

29. H. Schulweis, *op. cit.*

30. H. Gans, *op. cit.,* p. 14.

31. C. Silverman, *Congress Bi-weekly,* May 23, 1966, p. 7.

32. M.J. Rosenberg, *The Village Voice,* Feb. 13, 1969.

33. Deuteronomy 30:19.

Opinionaire on Race Relations

1. All men are endowed "with certain inalienable rights: among these are life, liberty, and the pursuit of happiness."
Agree strongly ( )   Disagree strongly ( )   Undecided ( )
Agree mildly ( )   Disagree mildly ( )

2. All Americans should be given equal opportunity to make the most of their talents and abilities.
Agree strongly ( )   Disagree strongly ( )   Undecided ( )
Agree mildly ( )   Disagree mildly ( )

3. It is almost impossible for a white person to be a really close friend of a Negro.
Agree strongly ( )   Disagree strongly ( )   Undecided ( )
Agree mildly ( )   Disagree mildly ( )

4. The attitude of whites towards blacks should not affect the black man's obligation to respect the rights of white people.
Agree strongly ( )   Disagree strongly ( )   Undecided ( )
Agree mildly ( )   Disagree mildly ( )

5. Most slumdwellers are where they are primarily because they lack the ambition or will power needed for success.
Agree strongly ( )   Disagree strongly ( )   Undecided ( )
Agree mildly ( )   Disagree mildly ( )

6. Under certain conditions, individuals may be justified in breaking laws to secure their human rights.
Agree strongly ( )   Disagree strongly ( )   Undecided ( )
Agree mildly ( )   Disagree mildly ( )

7. If black parents prefer black administrators in ghetto schools, then white administrators should stay out of such schools.
Agree strongly ( )   Disagree strongly ( )   Undecided ( )
Agree mildly ( )   Disagree mildly ( )

8. The attitude of blacks towards Jews should not affect the participation of the Jew in the struggle for justice for people of all races.
Agree strongly ( )   Disagree strongly ( )   Undecided ( )
Agree mildly ( )   Disagree mildly ( )

9. Since the Jews lifted themselves out of poverty by an emphasis on study and hard work, the American Negro should be able to do the same.
Agree strongly ( )   Disagree strongly ( )   Undecided ( )
Agree mildly ( )   Disagree mildly ( )

10. When Negroes move into a white neighborhood, the property values of the houses do not necessarily fall.
Agree strongly ( )   Disagree strongly ( )   Undecided ( )
Agree mildly ( )   Disagree mildly ( )

11. Intermarriage between the races is harmful, because it will lead eventually to the disappearance of the white civilization.
Agree strongly ( )   Disagree strongly ( )   Undecided ( )
Agree mildly ( )   Disagree mildly ( )

12. Intermarriage between the races is harmful, because society will make life miserable for the children.

Agree strongly ( )   Disagree strongly ( )   Undecided ( )
Agree mildly ( )   Disagree mildly ( )

13. Schools in slum neighborhoods should receive special funds to set up free nursery schools and other remedial programs for their disadvantaged children.

Agree strongly ( )   Disagree strongly ( )   Undecided ( )
Agree mildly ( )   Disagree mildly ( )

14. A man has the right to sell his house or to refuse to sell his house to anyone he pleases.

Agree strongly ( )   Disagree strongly ( )   Undecided ( )
Agree mildly ( )   Disagree mildly ( )

15. Sometimes twice as much money is spent for the education of the pupil in the suburban school as is spent on the education of the slum child in the nearby city. This situation is unfair and should be corrected.

Agree strongly ( )   Disagree strongly ( )   Undecided ( )
Agree mildly ( )   Disagree mildly ( )

16. The Negro should show a higher level of responsibility as a law-abiding citizen than he has shown thus far if he wants to receive equal rights.

Agree strongly ( )   Disagree strongly ( )   Undecided ( )
Agree mildly ( )   Disagree mildly ( )

17. It is legitimate to demand that a firm that has never employed Negroes must hire a certain number within a given period of time.

Agree strongly ( )   Disagree strongly ( )   Undecided ( )
Agree mildly ( )   Disagree mildly ( )

18. Black parents have a right to determine policies affecting budget, curriculum, and personnel in the schools to which they send their children.

Agree strongly ( )   Disagree strongly ( )   Undecided ( )
Agree mildly ( )   Disagree mildly ( )

19. Integration of schools and neighborhoods is undesirable because such steps will inevitably lead to intermarriage.

Agree strongly ( )   Disagree strongly ( )   Undecided ( )
Agree mildly ( )   Disagree mildly ( )

20. If laws were passed enabling Negroes to move into white neighborhoods, then eventually greater understanding would develop among people living in the "mixed" areas.

Agree strongly ( )   Disagree strongly ( )   Undecided ( )
Agree mildly ( )   Disagree mildly ( )

21. Because Jews have known what discrimination means, they should feel particularly sympathetic to the American Negro.

Agree strongly ( )   Disagree strongly ( )   Undecided ( )
Agree mildly ( )   Disagree mildly ( )

ABOUT
THE AUTHOR

HENRY COHEN was born in Texas, where his grandfather, great grandfather, and uncle were rabbis and among the pioneers of American Reform Judaism. His involvement with the struggle for equal rights began in the early 1950's when, as a rabbinic student at the Hebrew Union College, he was a participant in a "nonviolent direct action group" that succeeded in opening Cincinnati's music schools to Negroes. Before entering the college, he was graduated Phi Beta Kappa from the University of Texas. He served as chaplain in Korea and occupied pulpits in New York and Illinois. In 1964 he became spiritual leader of Beth David Reform Congregation, Philadelphia, Pa., where, he is pleased to report, his congregation "has had the courage to remodel its facilities in an integrating area of Philadelphia rather than follow the exodus to the suburbs." He holds an M.A. in Philosophy of Education from the University of Illinois, and has contributed articles to educational journals.

Rabbi Cohen is vice president of the Western Division of the Jewish Community Relations Council of Philadelphia, and is a member of the Commission on Decentralization and Community Participation of the School District of Philadelphia. He is married to Edna Goldzweig, a fourth-generation *sabra,* and they have two children, Shelley and Lisa.